I0499692

ANTI STRESS MANDALAS

Overcome Fear With Attractive Mandala Design Pattern

Mandala Craft Art

Copyright © 2019 by Mandala Craft Art

All Rights Reserved. No part of this publication may be reproduced, distributed, or transmitted in any form or by any means, including photocopying, recording, or other electronic or mechanical methods.

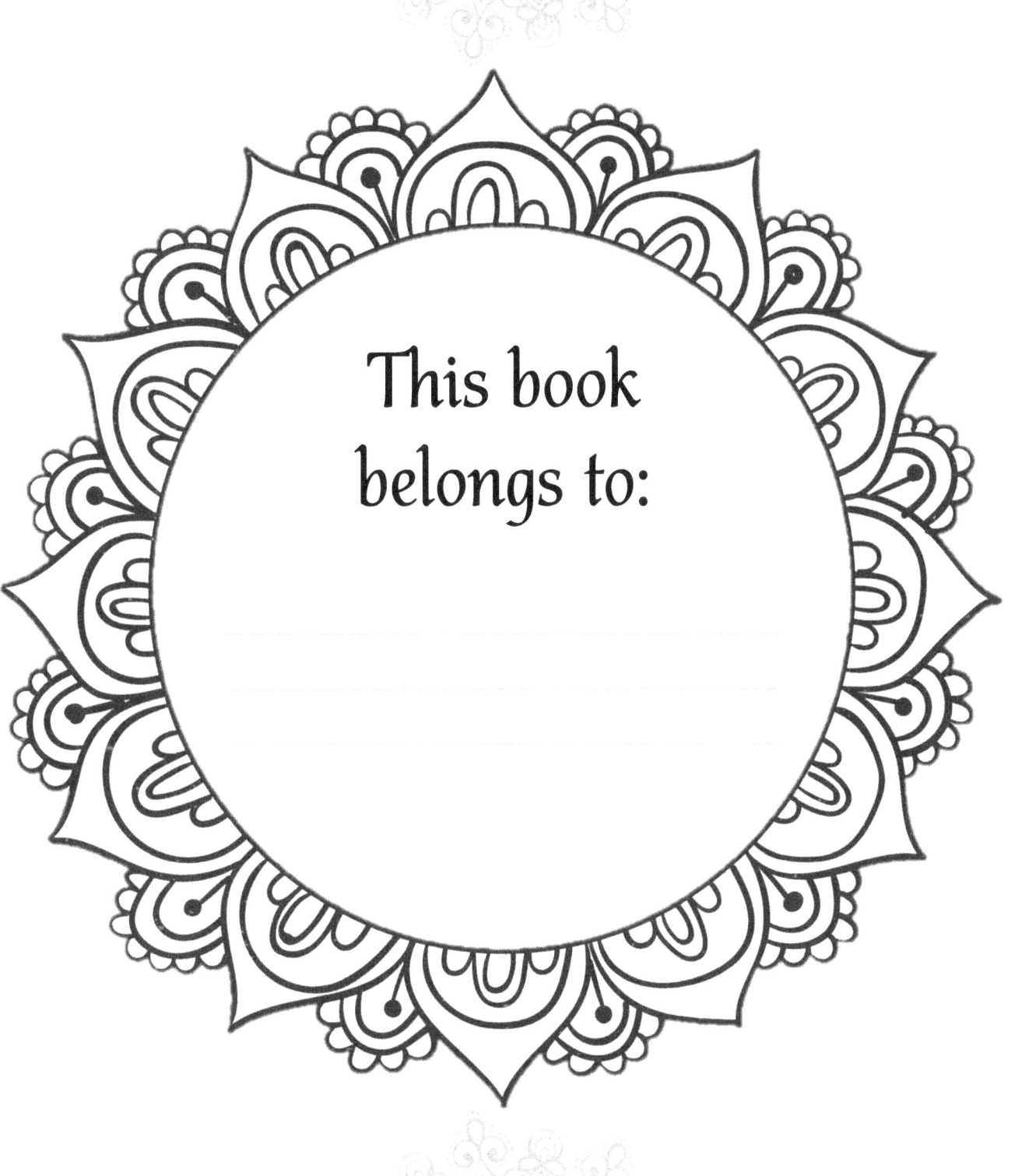

This book
belongs to:

Color Swatch

Test your color supplies on this page to see how they react to the paper. Place a blank page or two behind each page as your color, to prevent bleed-through to the next page.

Color this mandala!

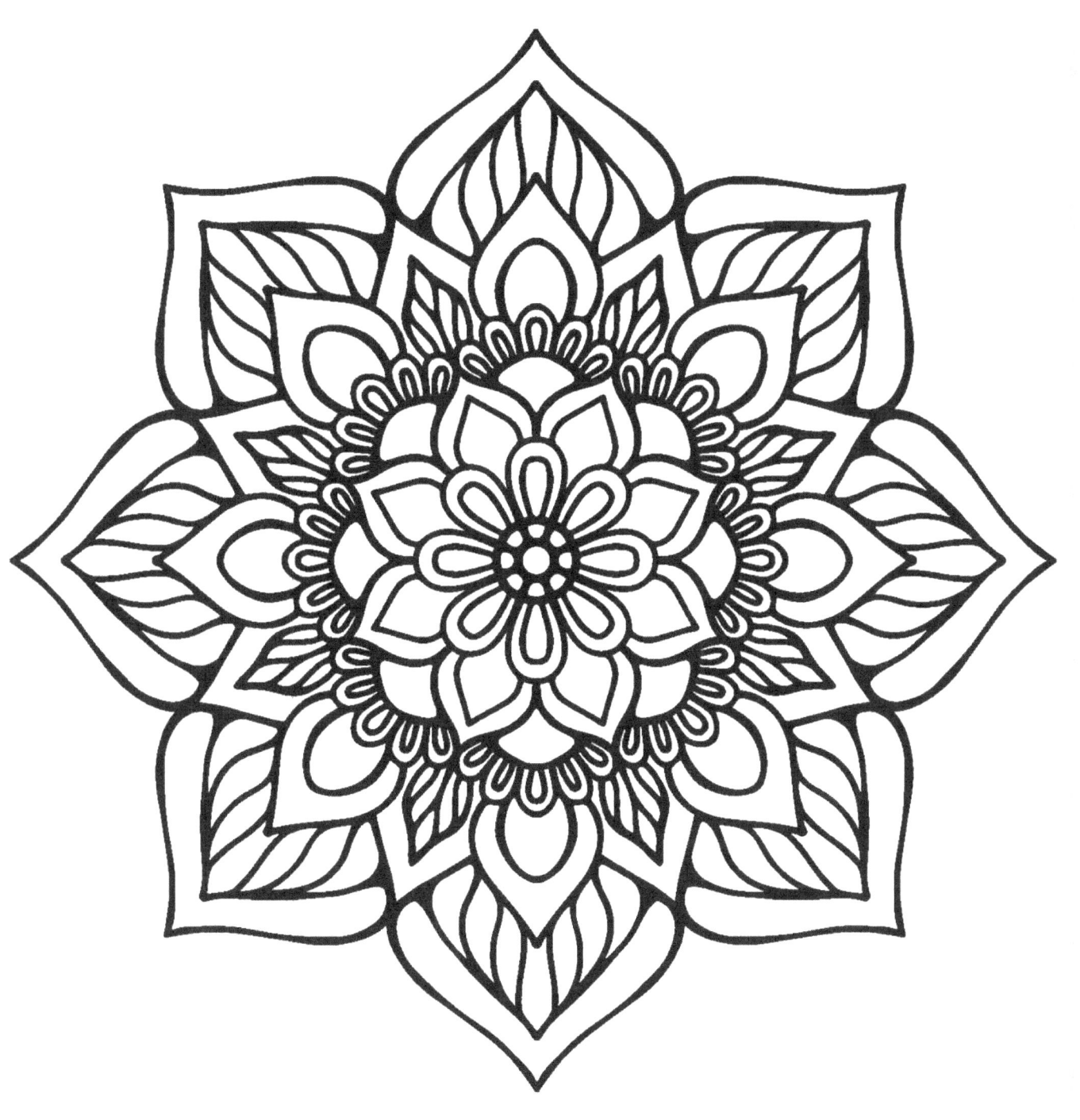

Color this mandala!

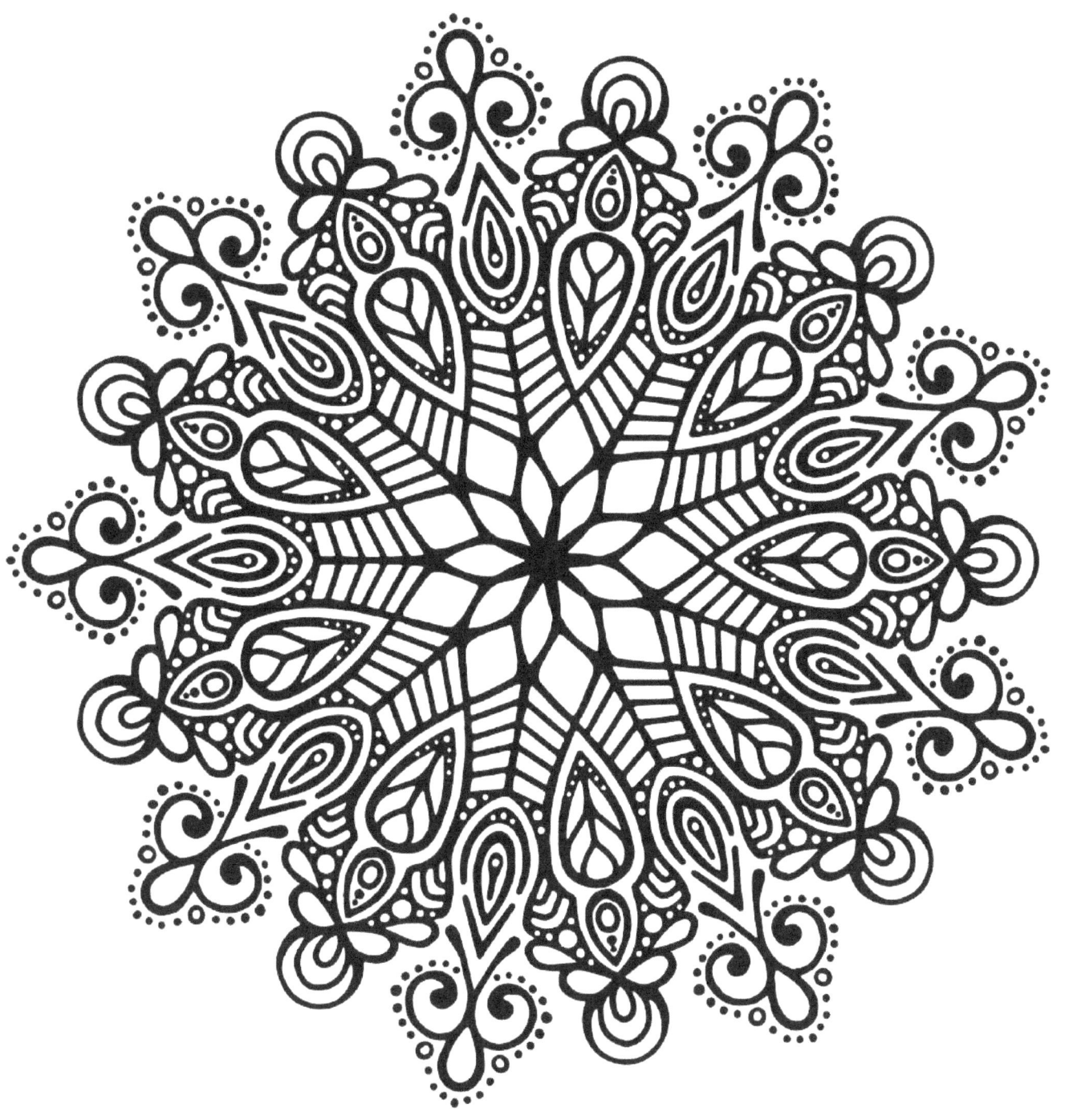

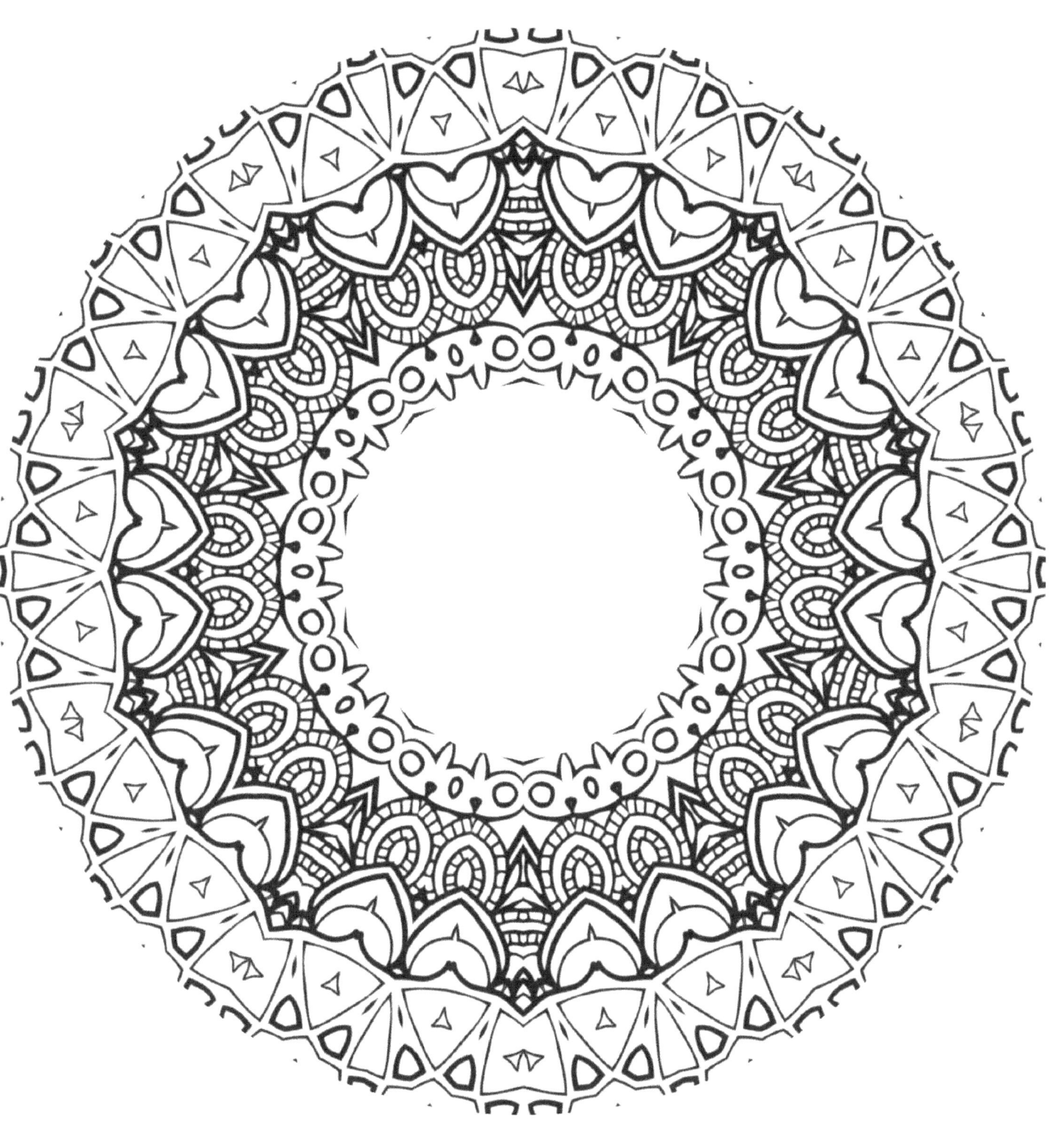

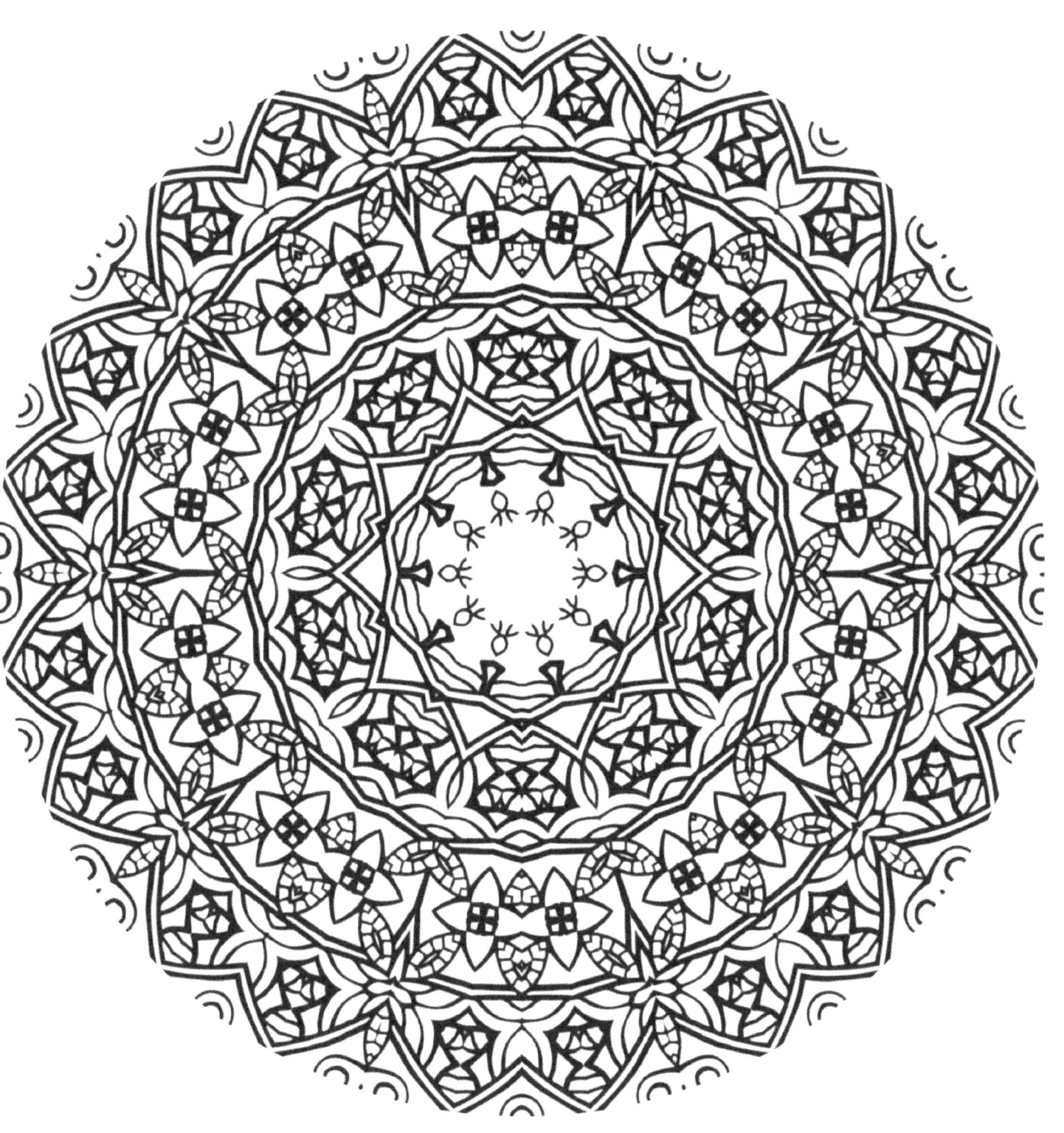

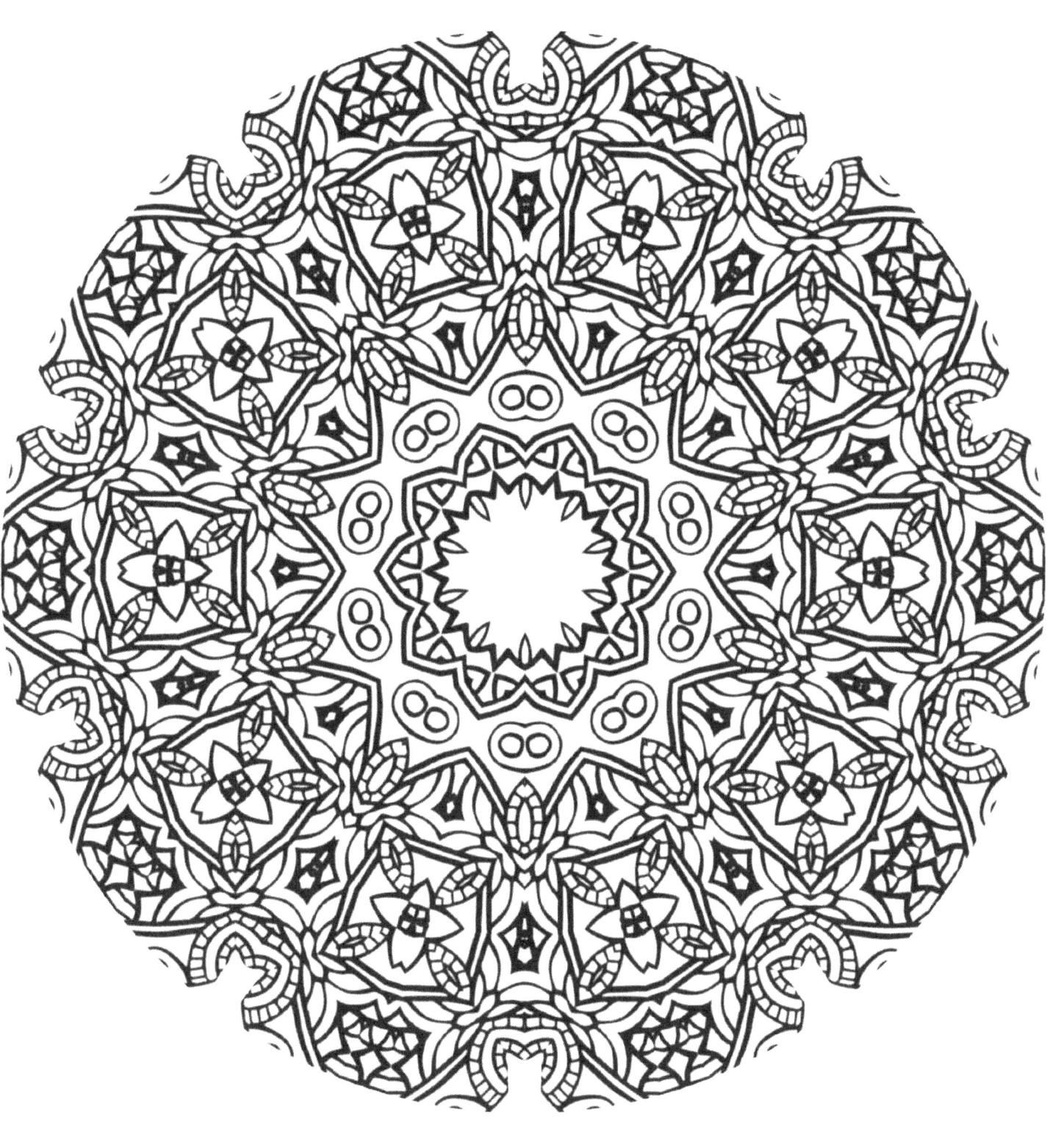

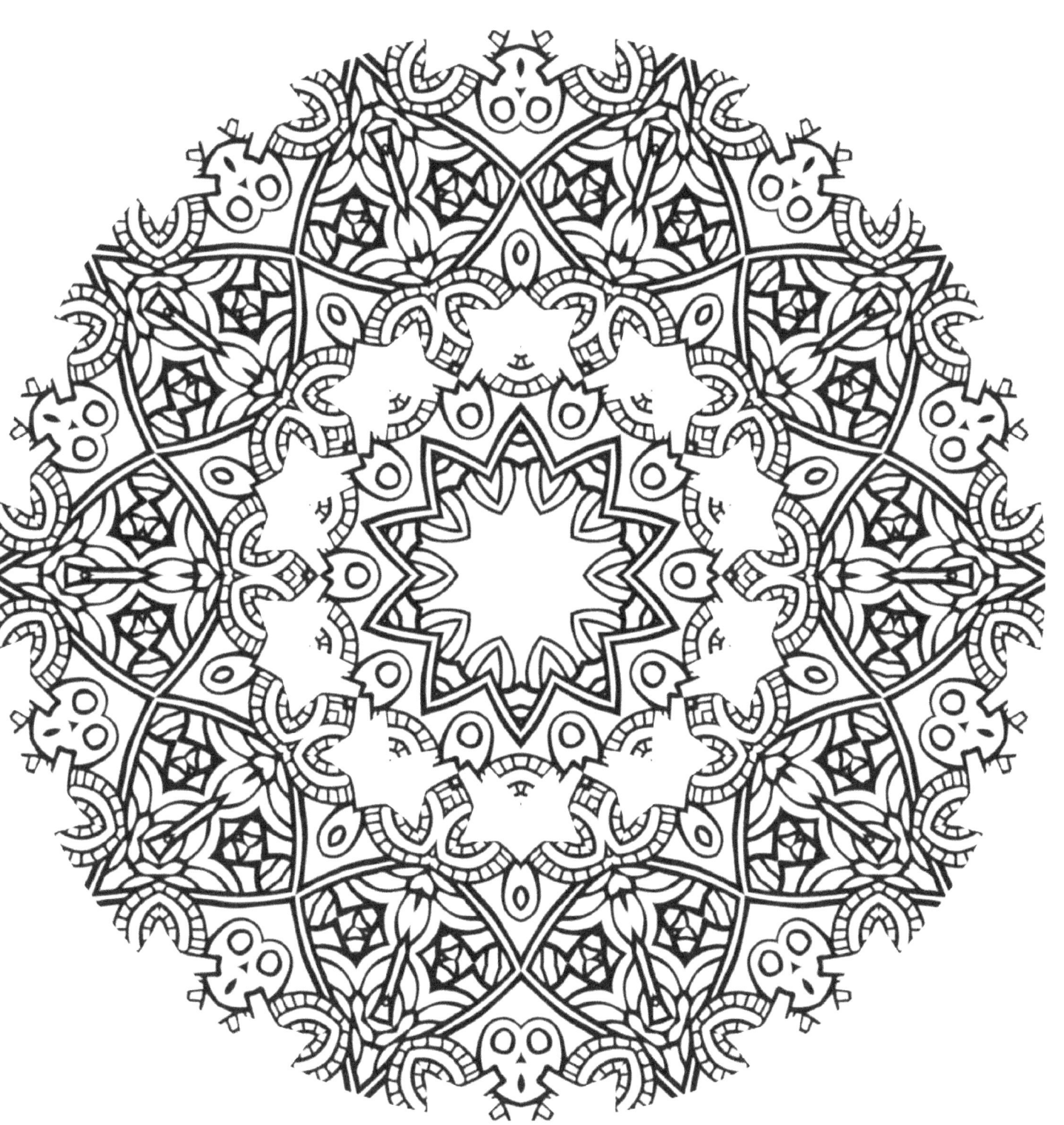

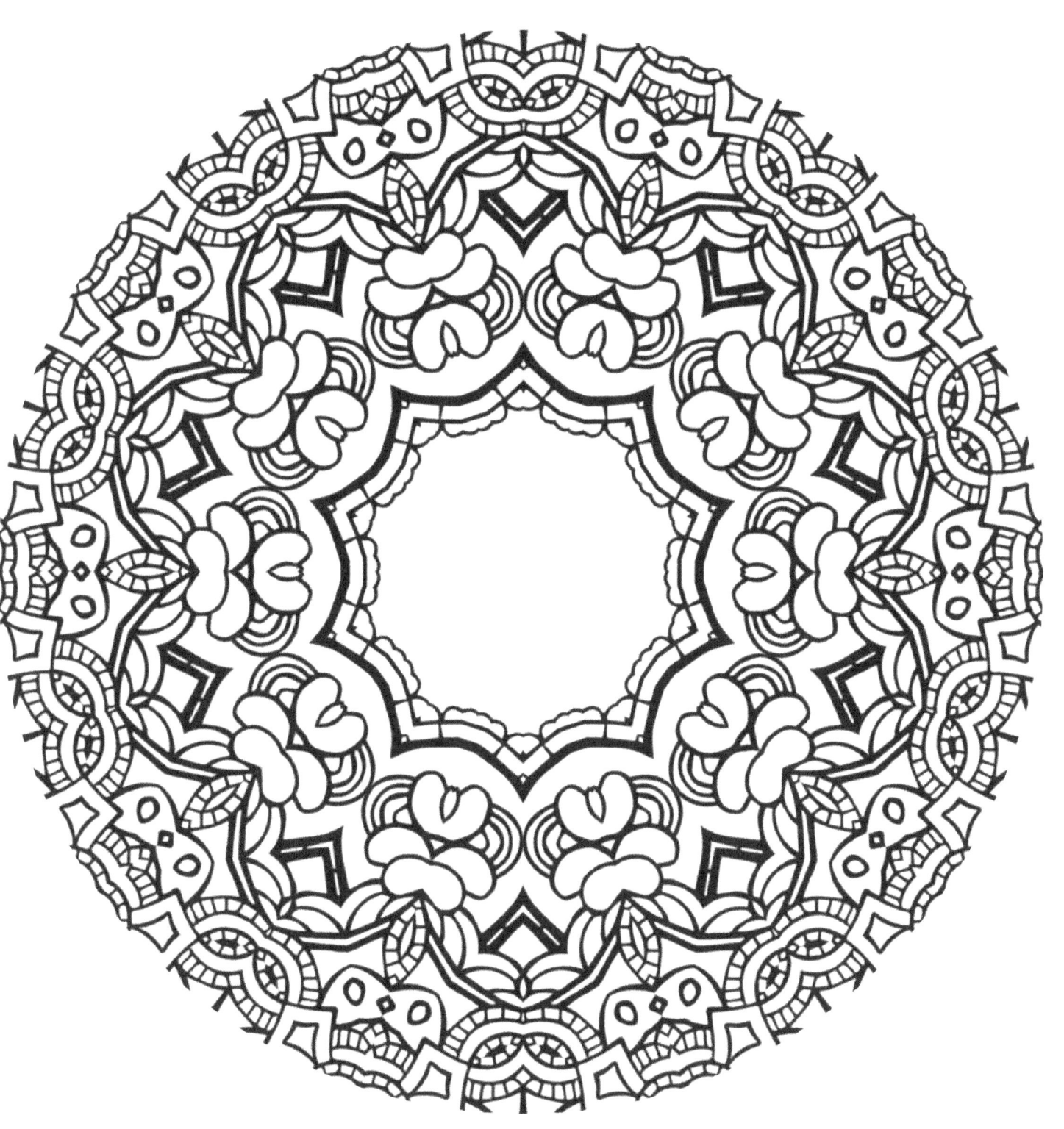

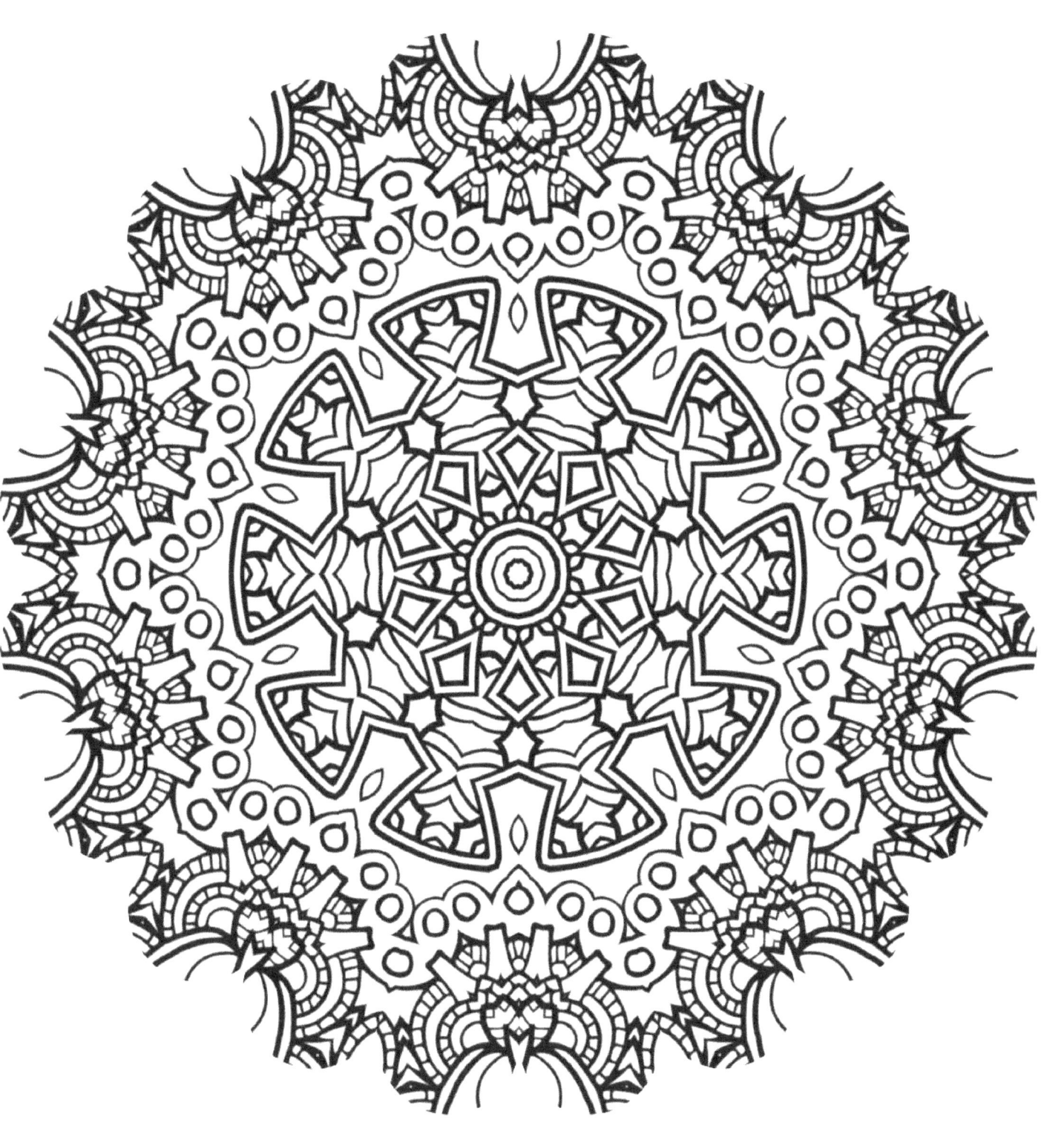

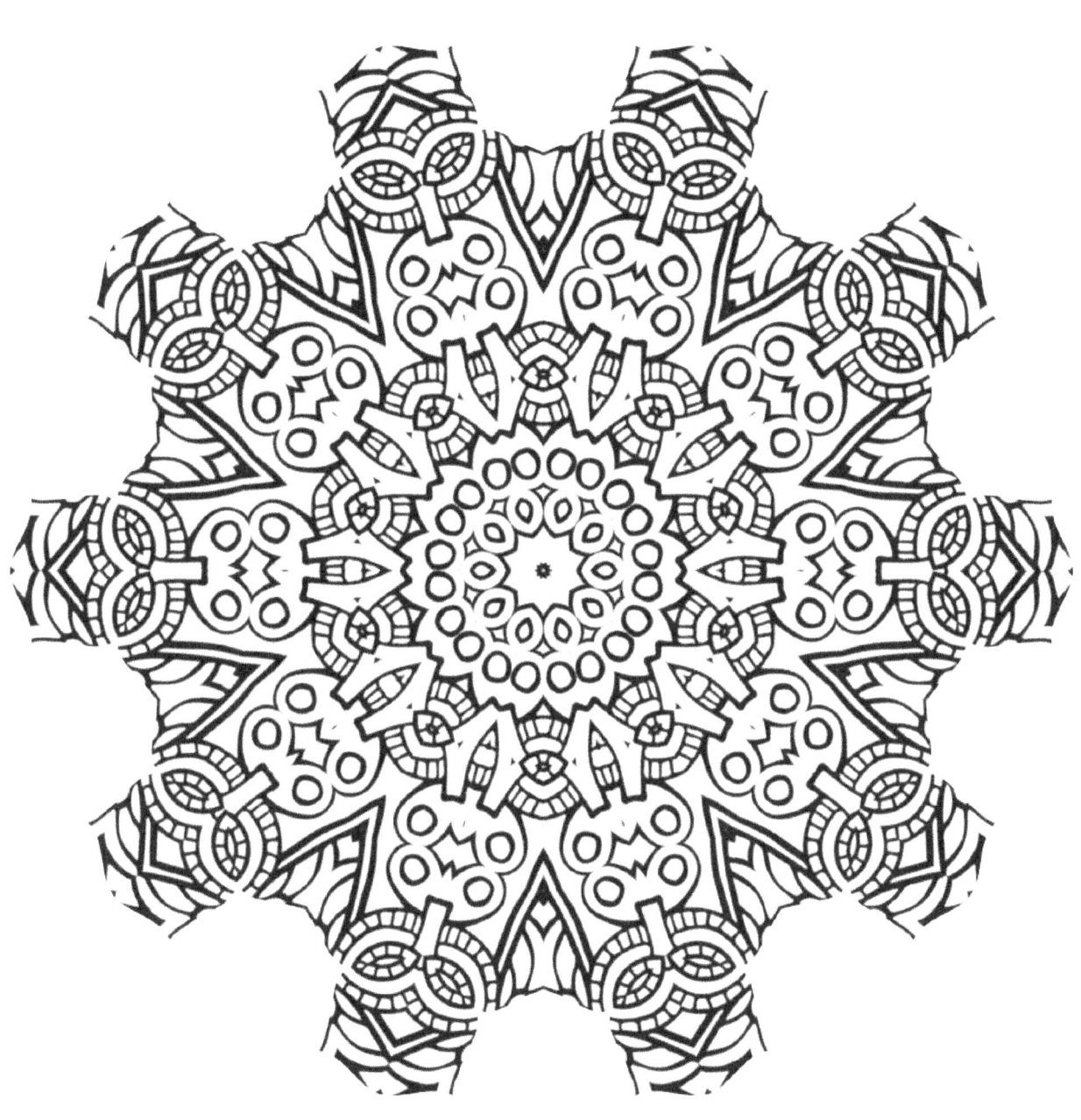

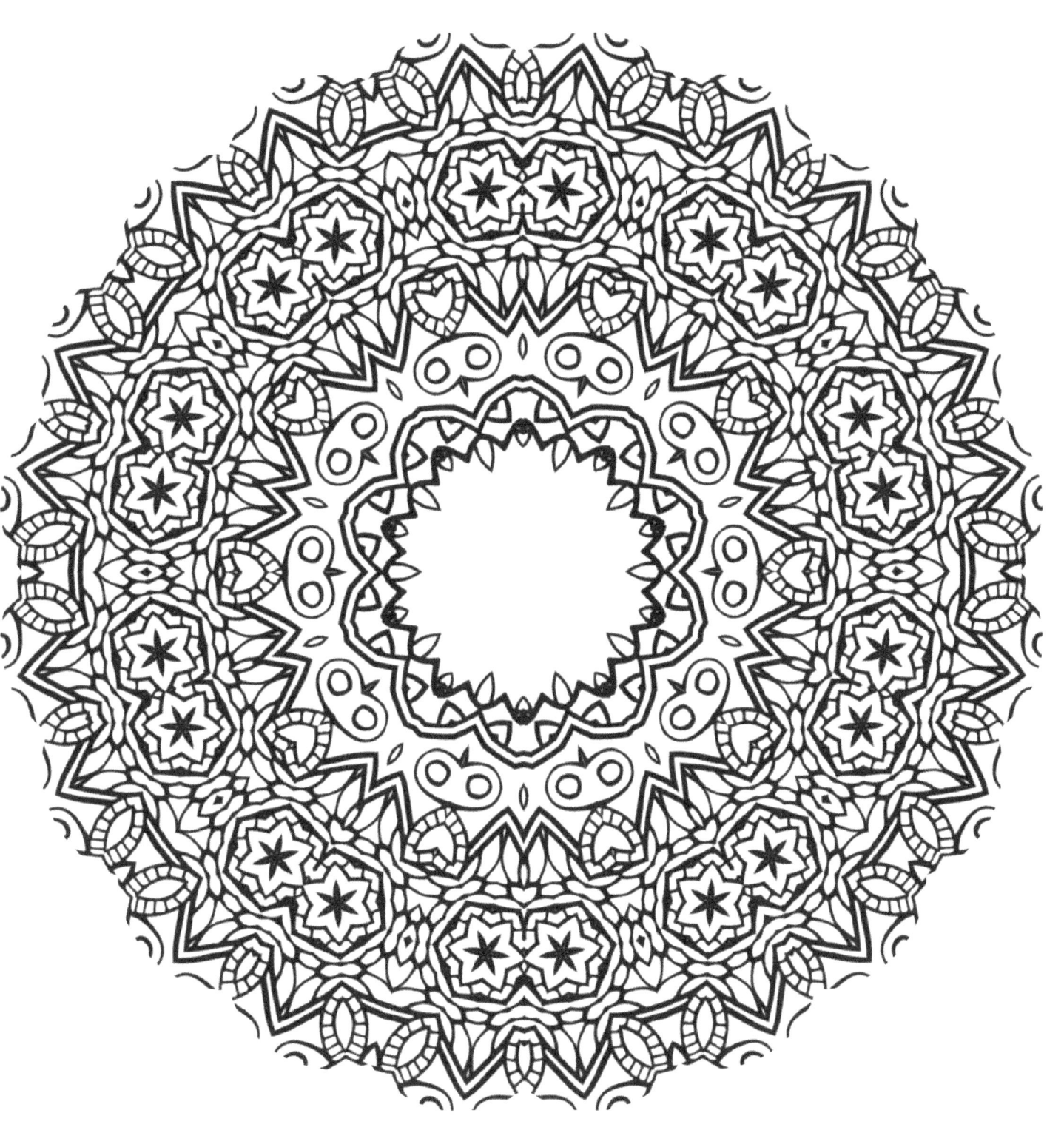

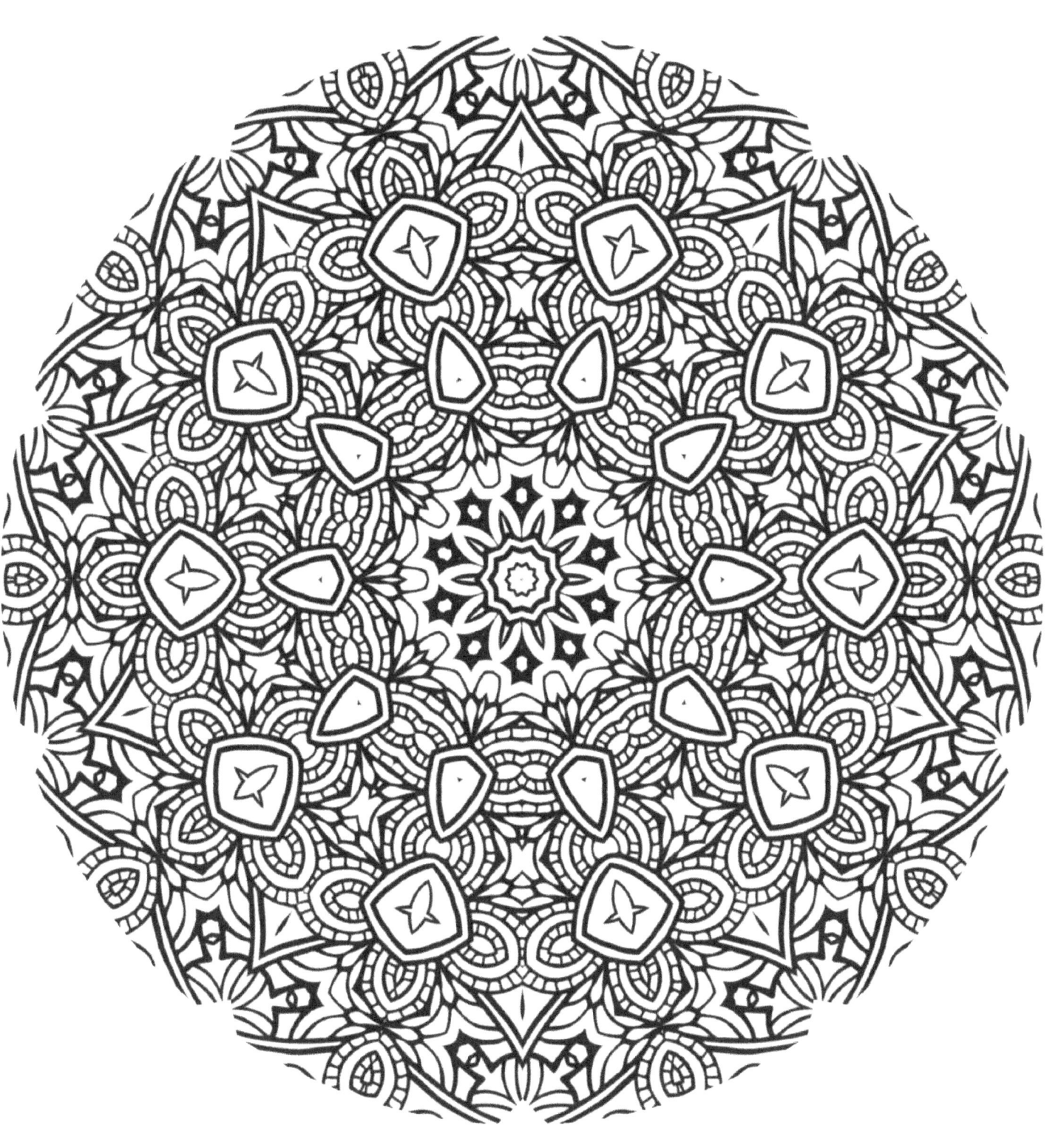

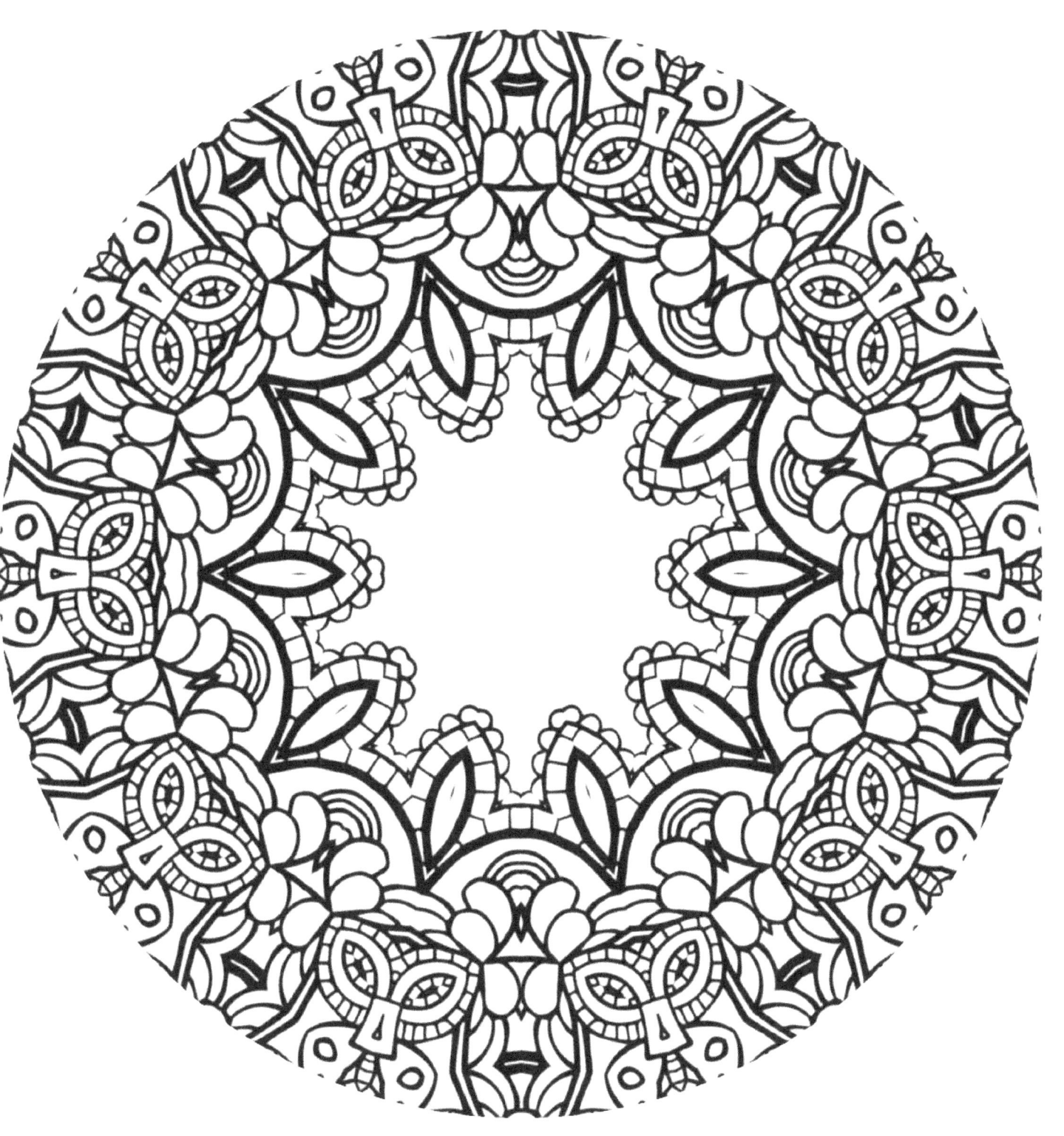

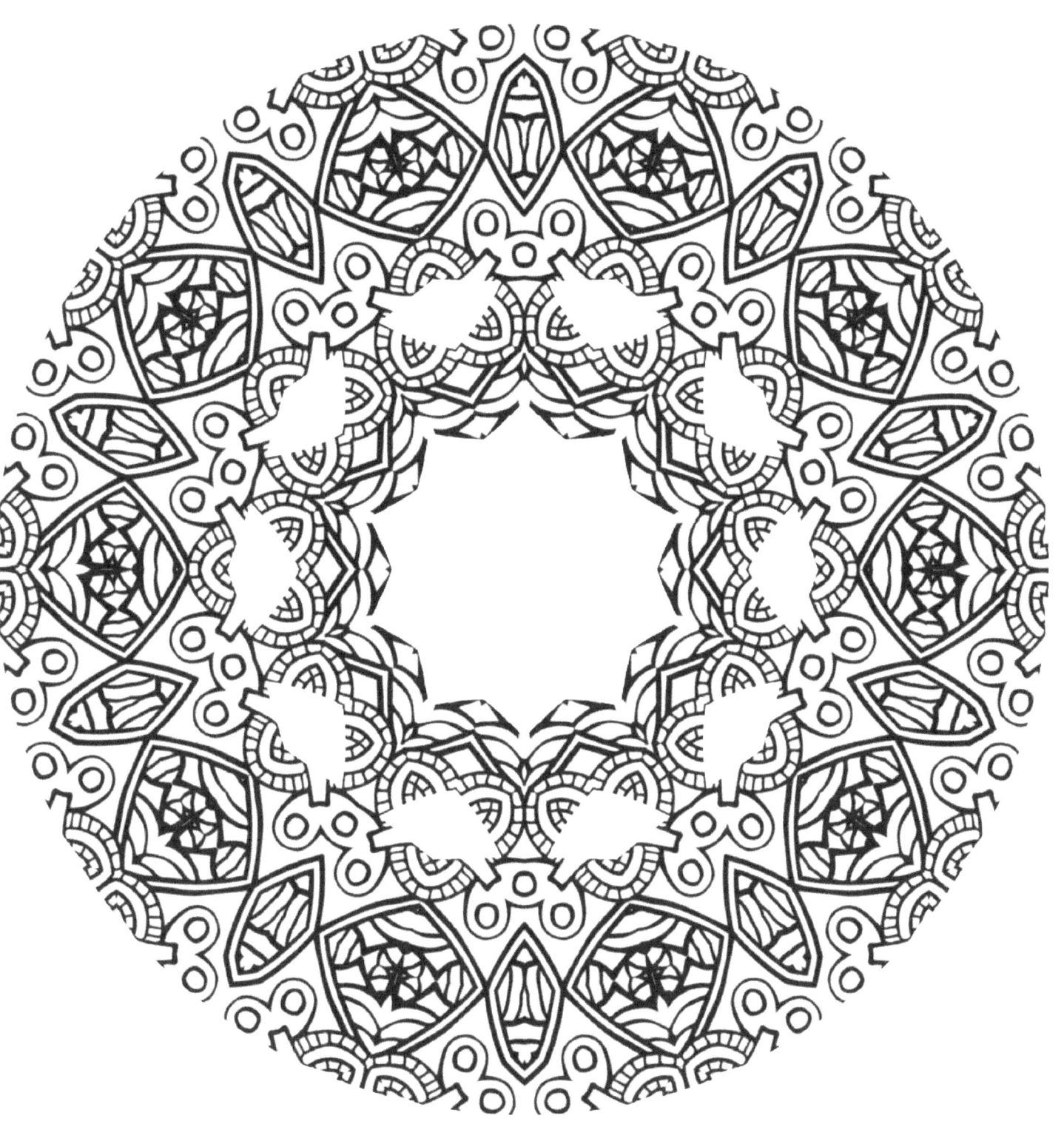

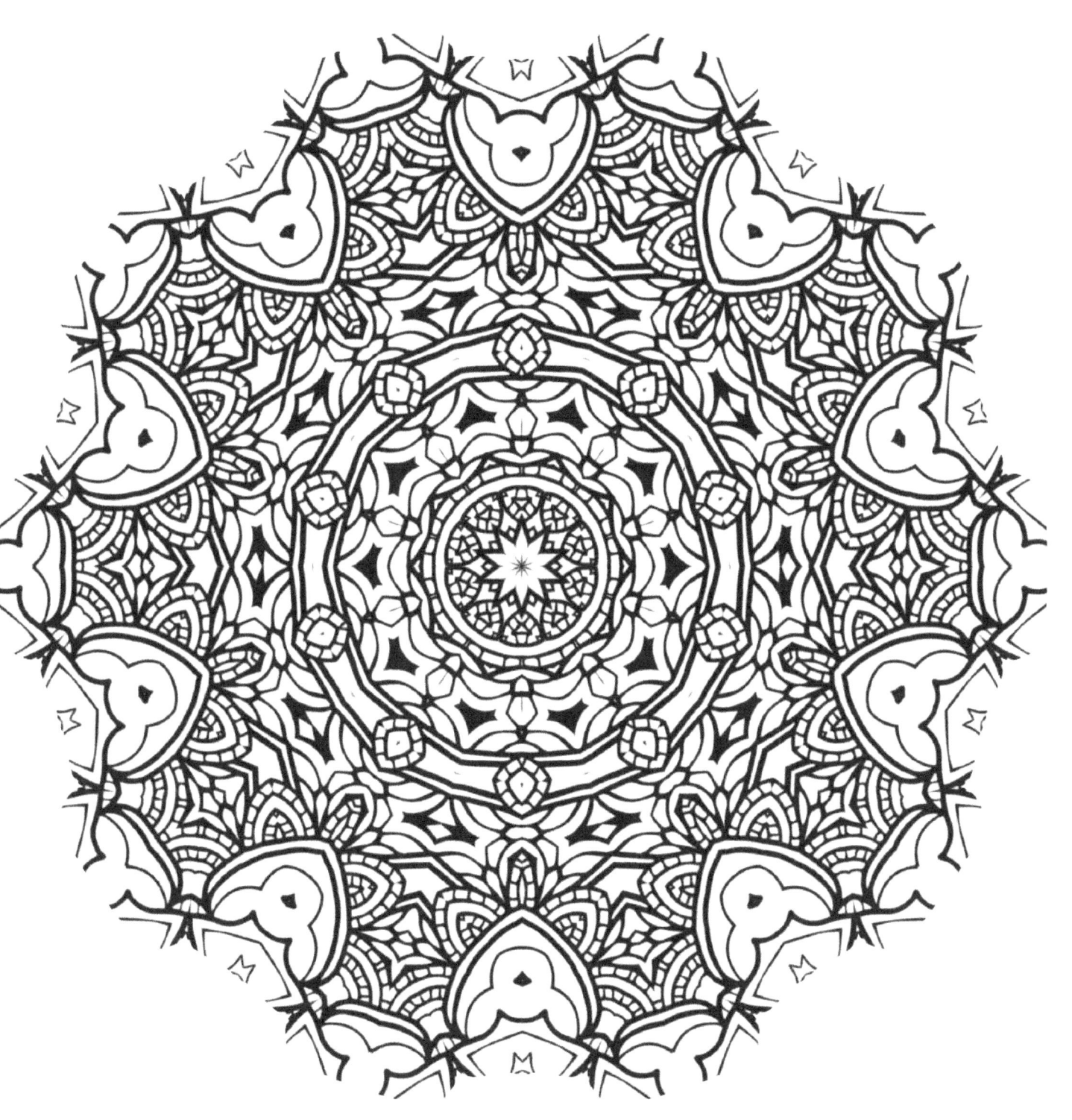

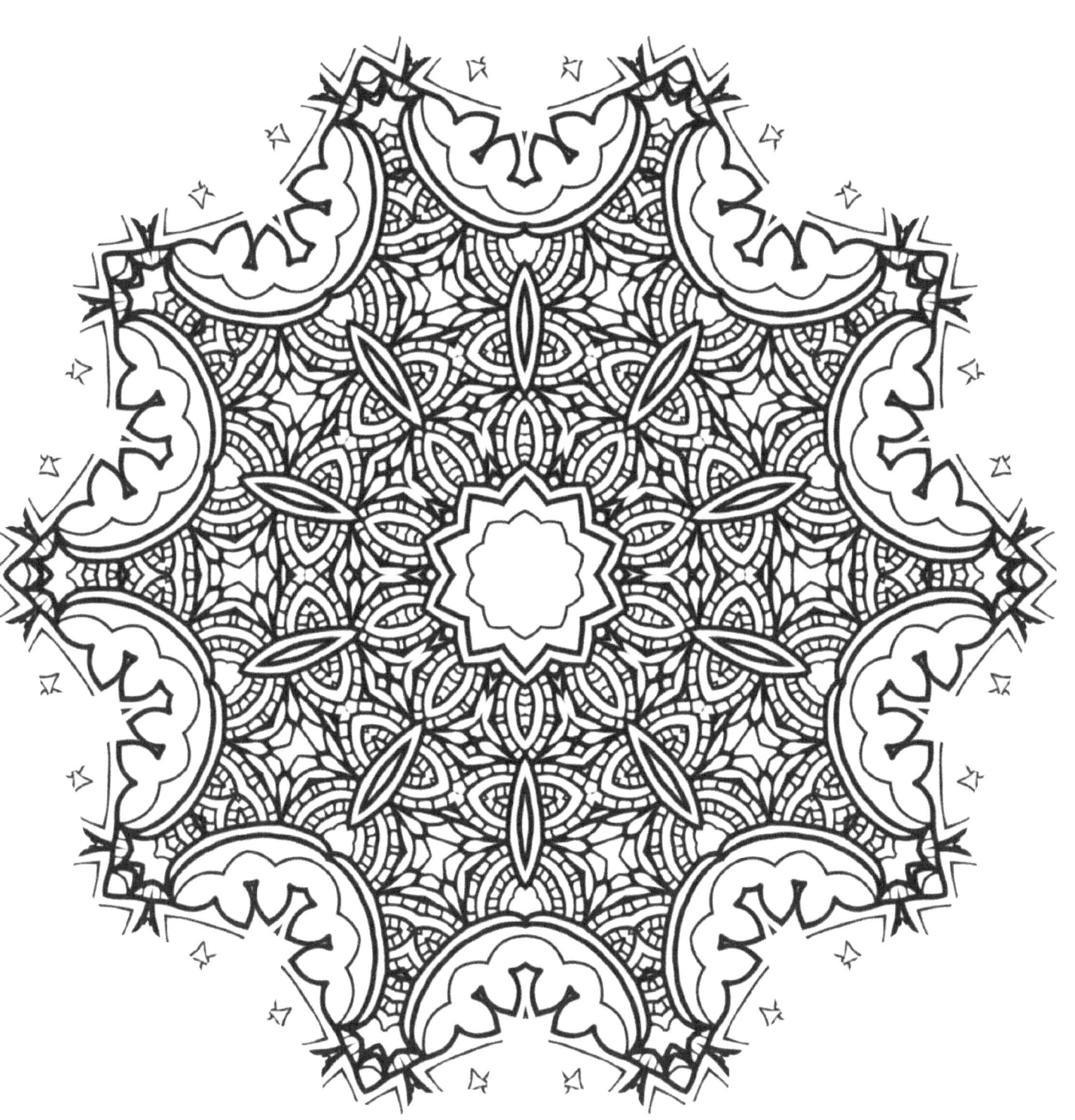

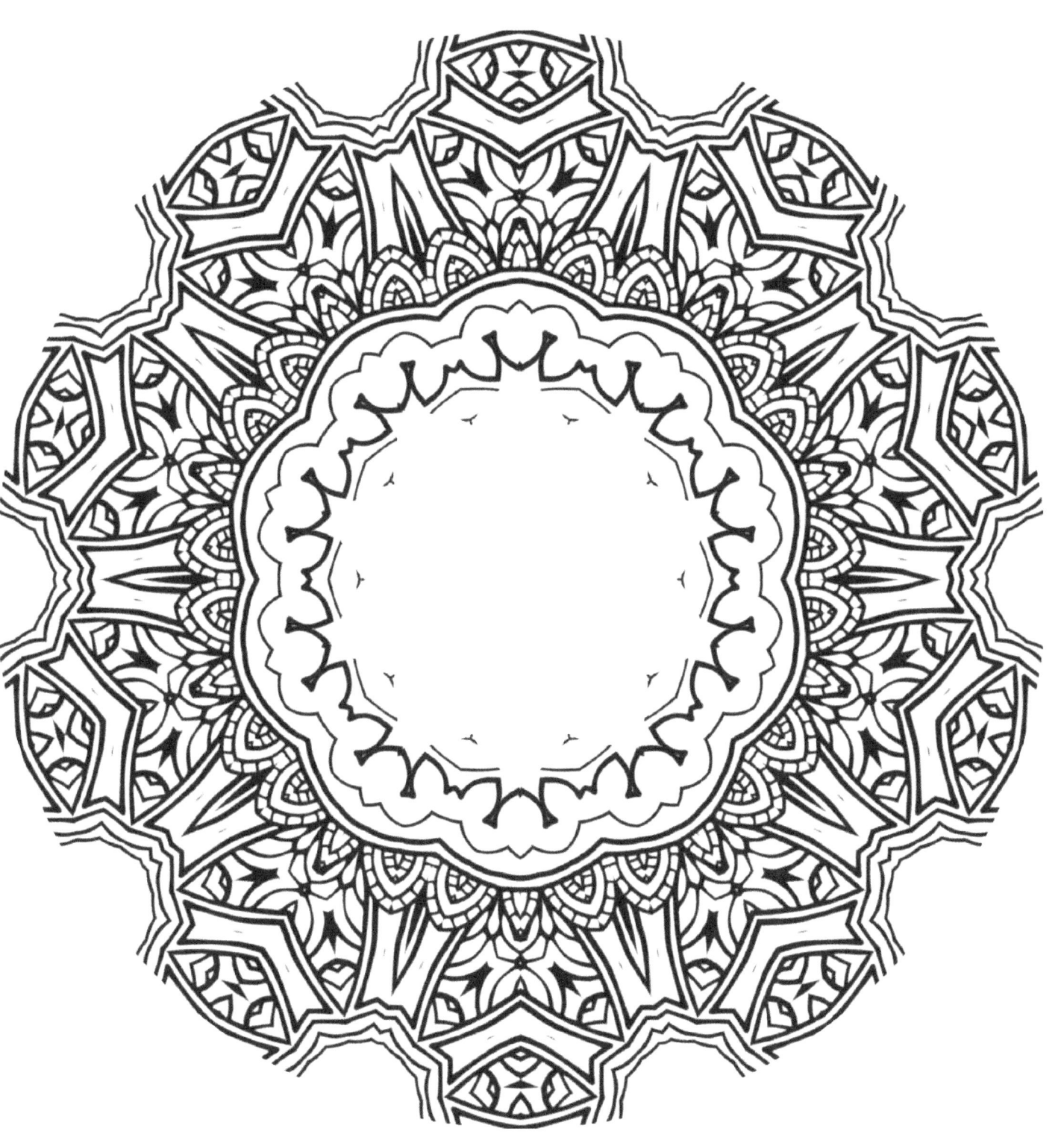

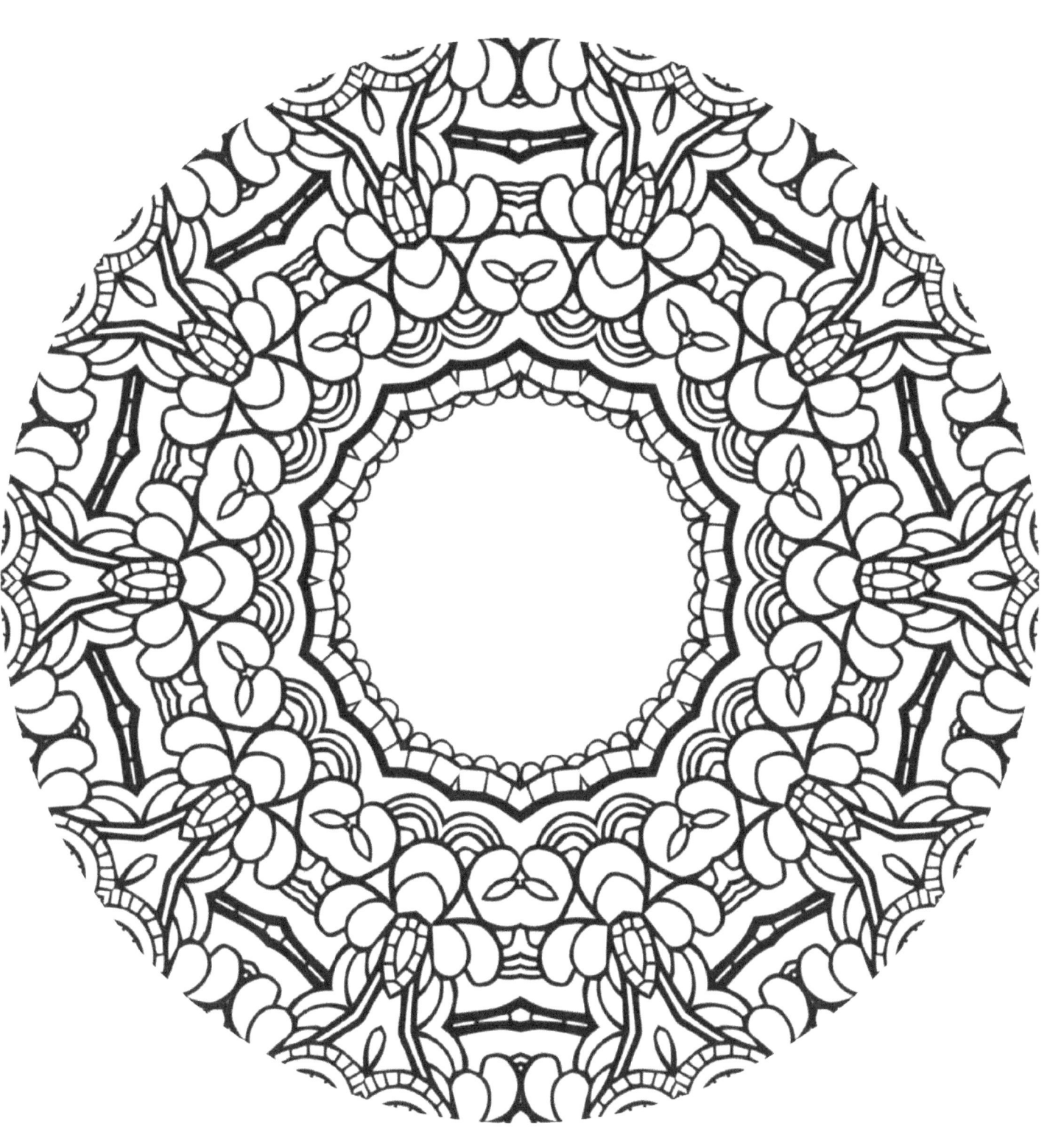

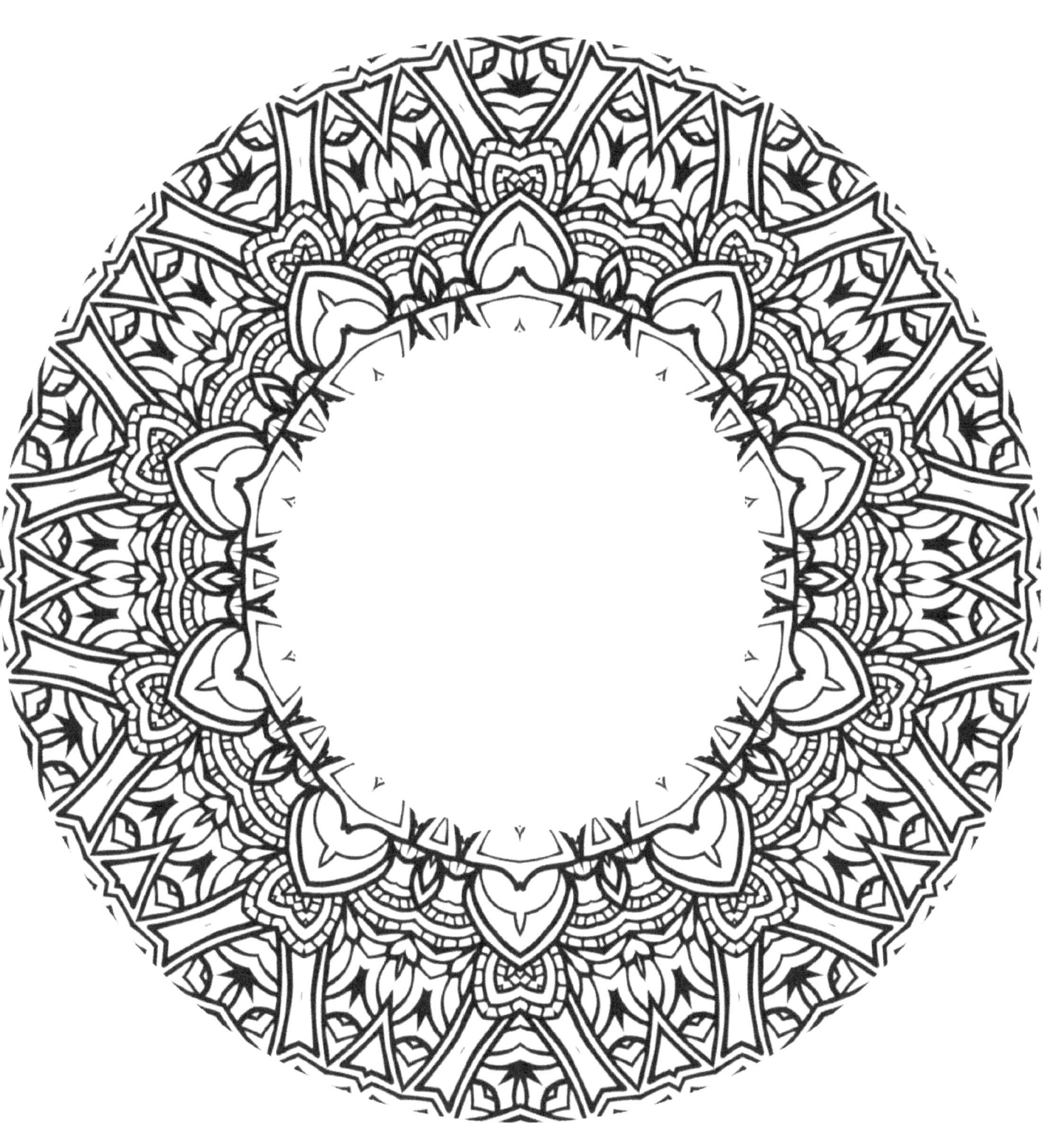

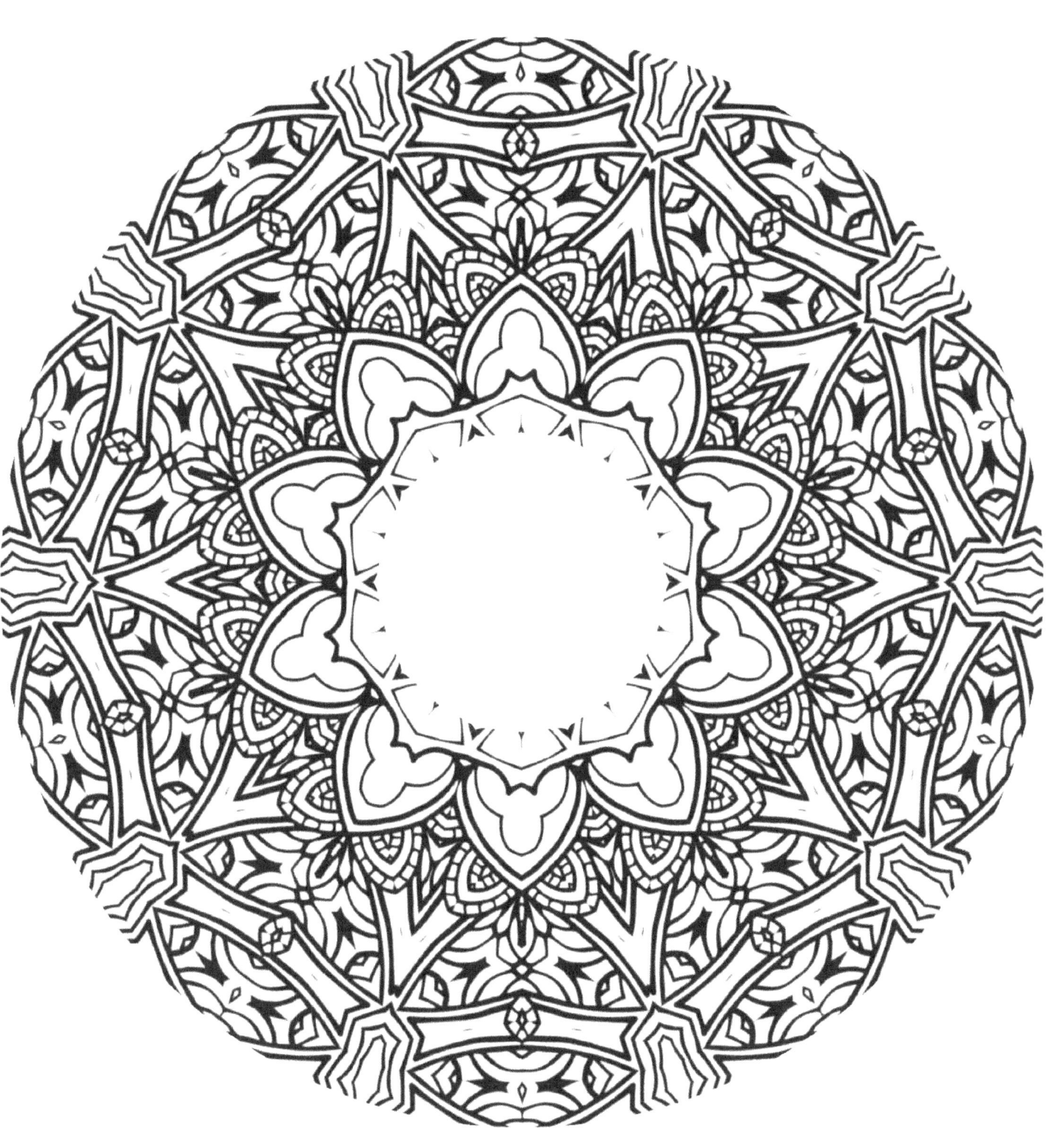

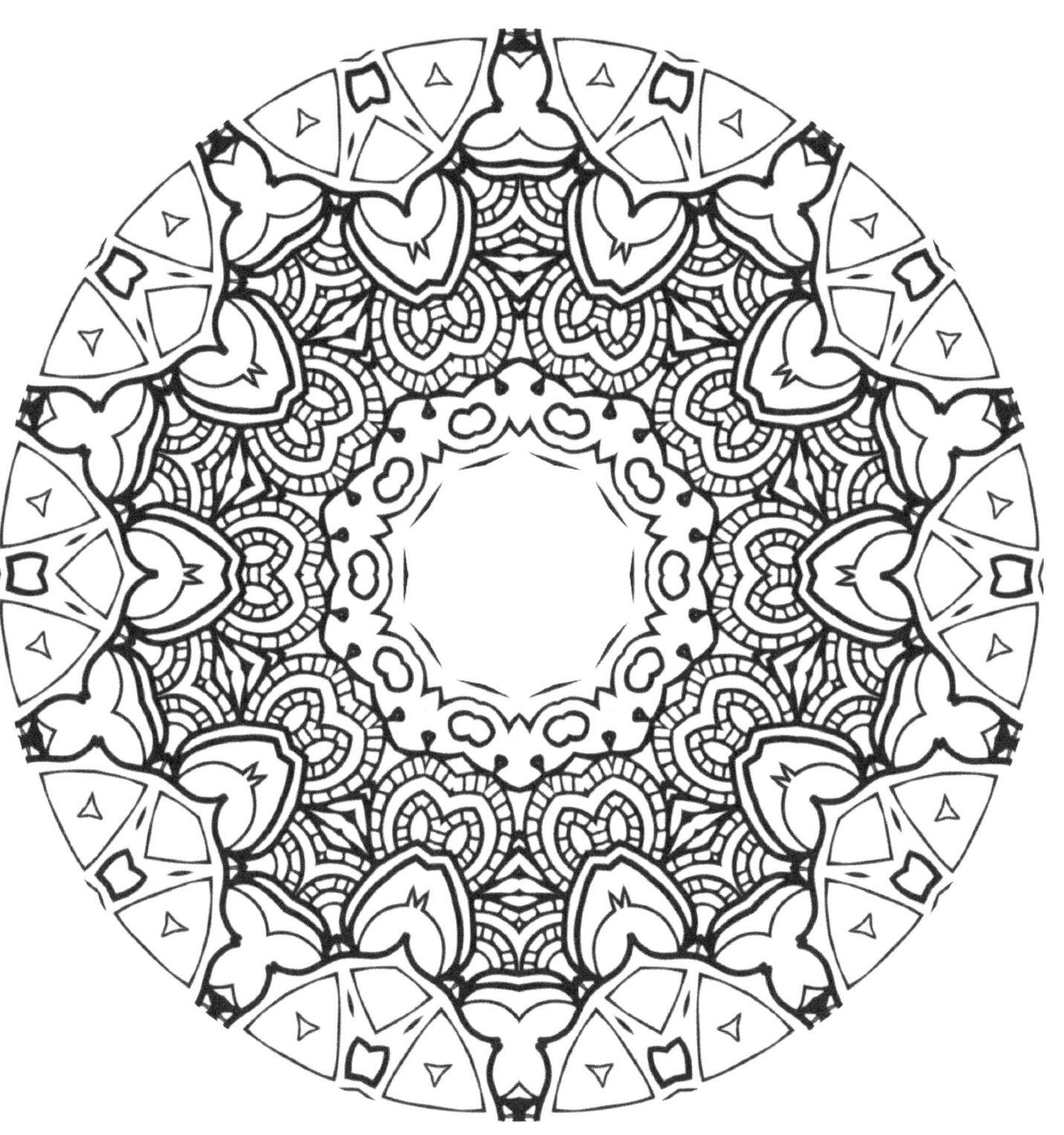

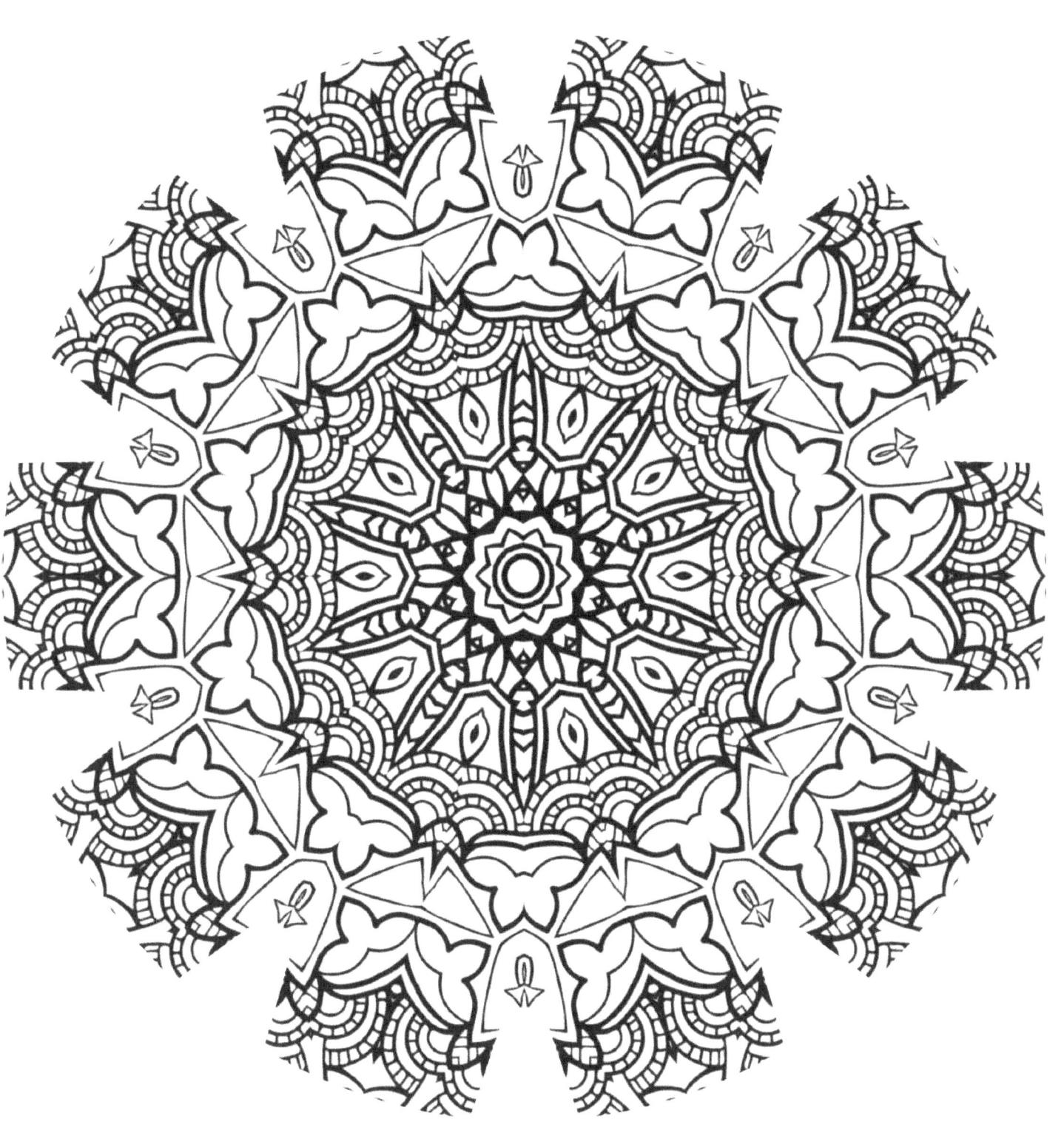

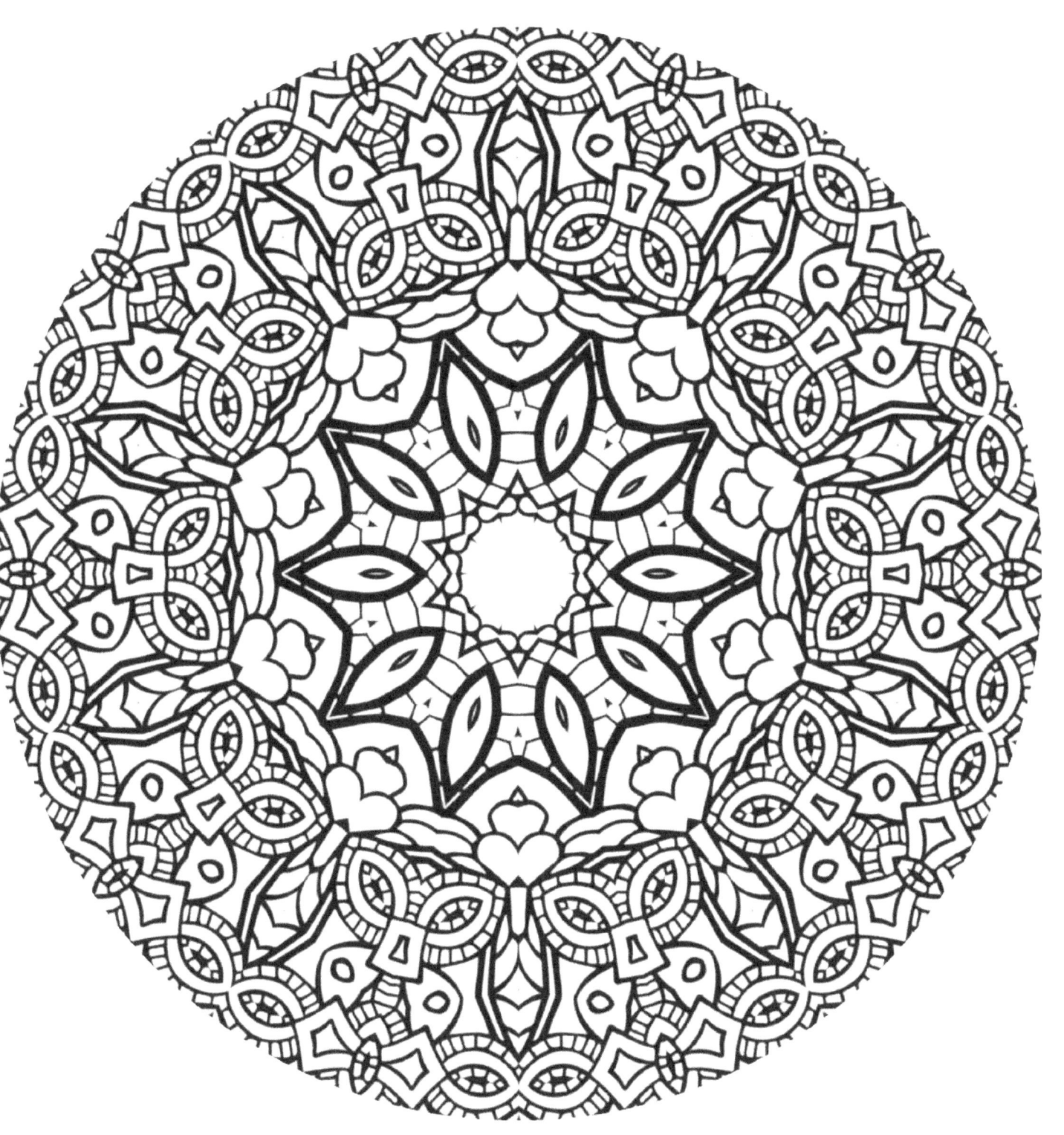

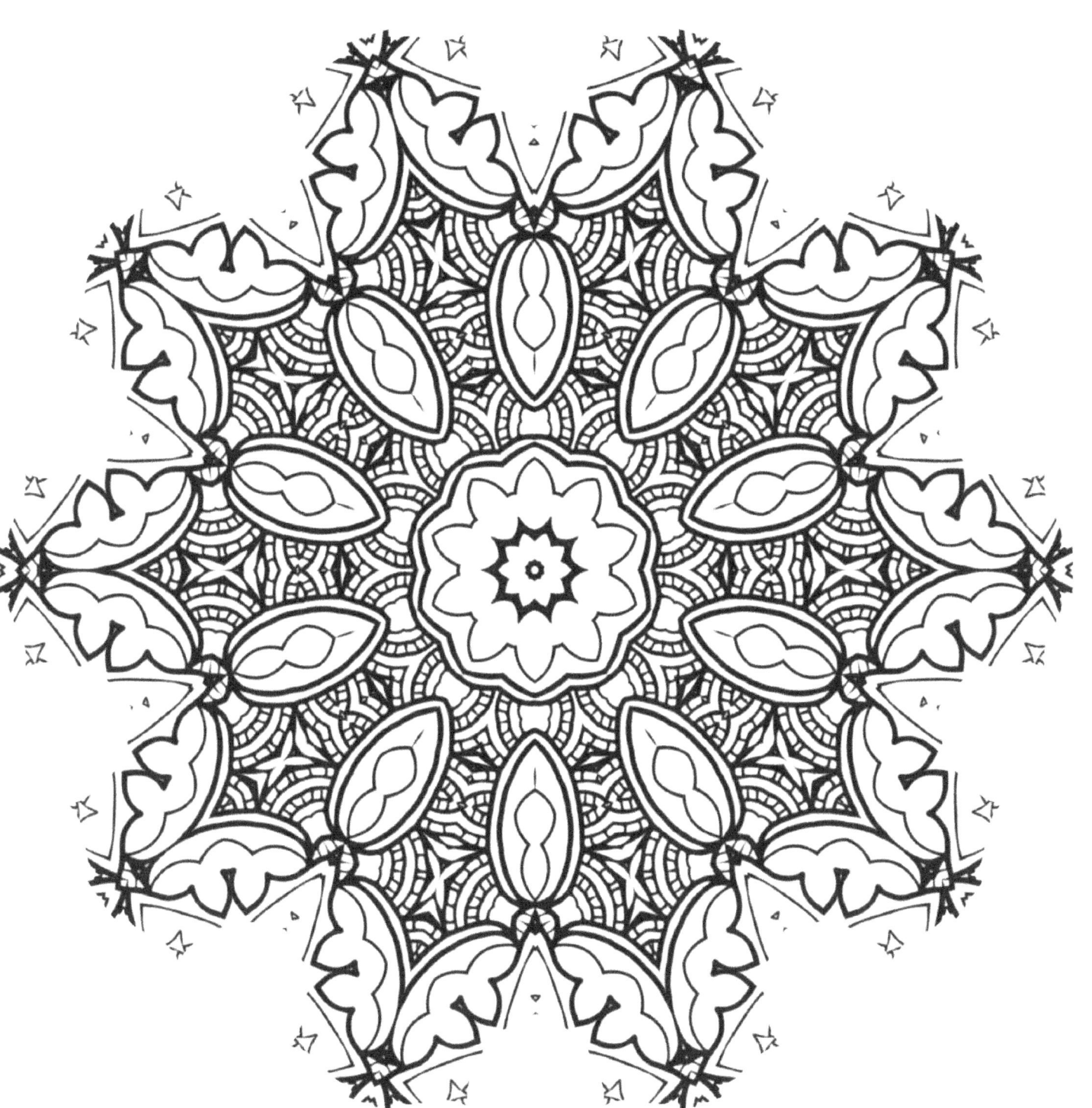

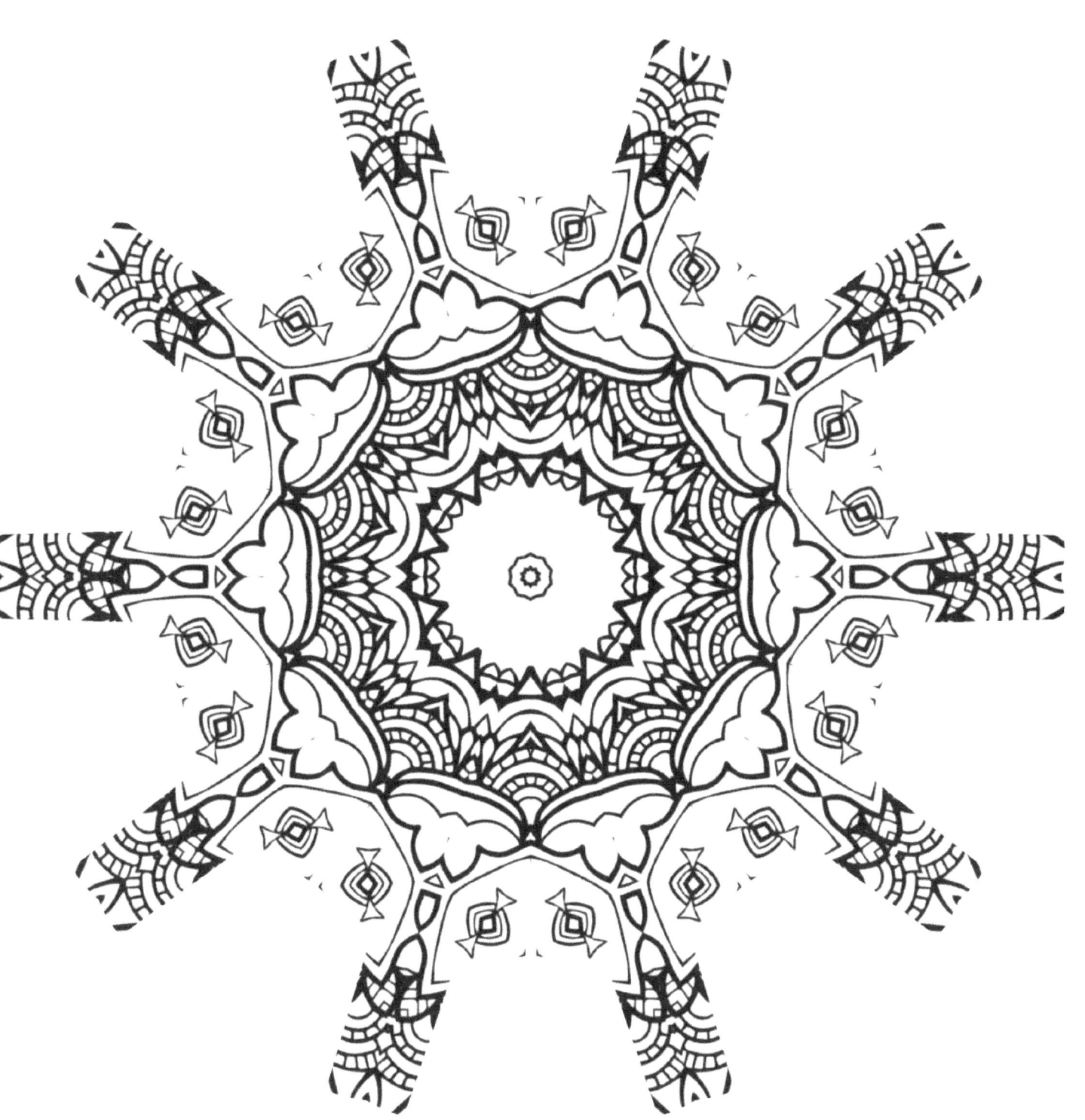

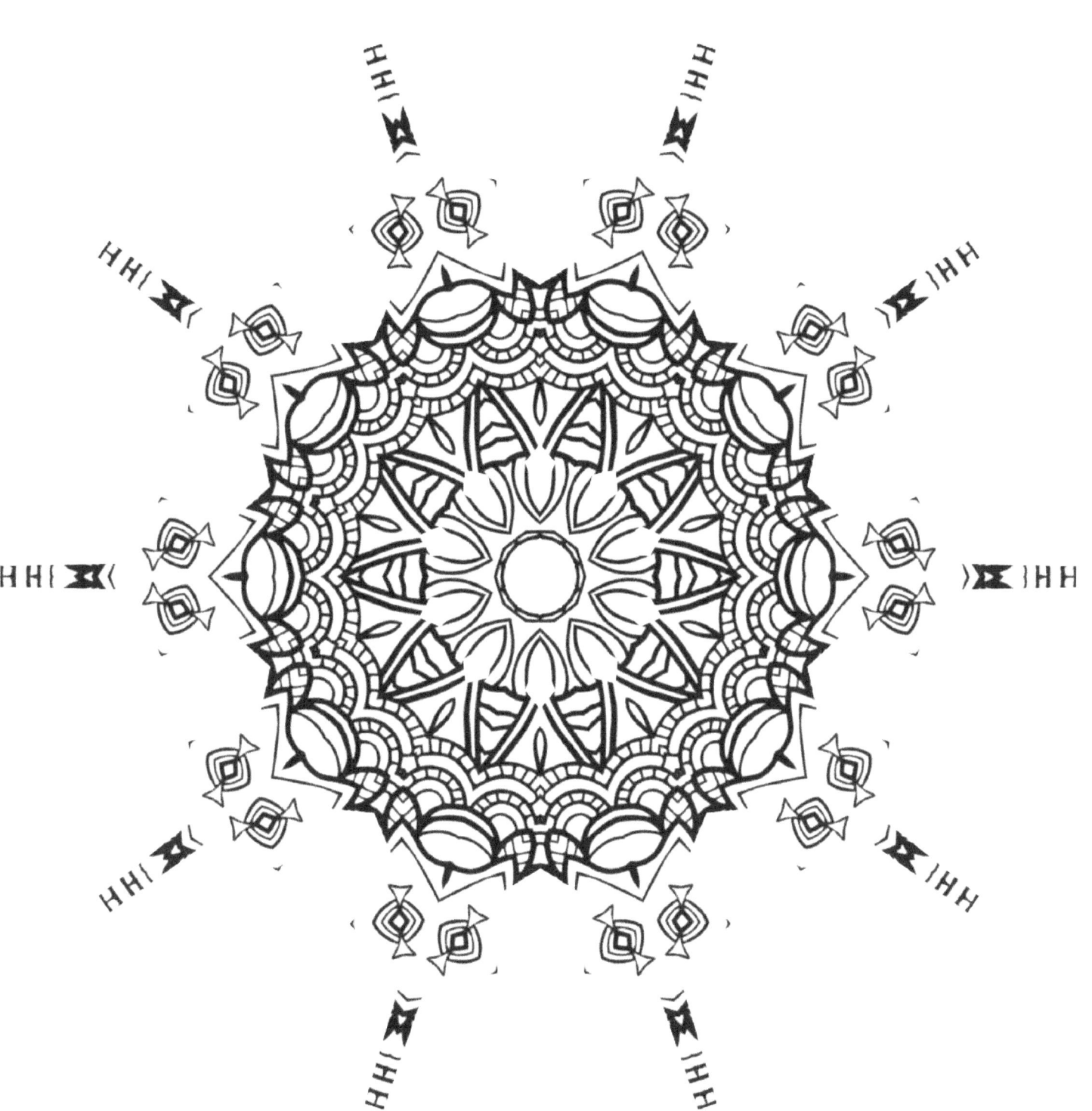

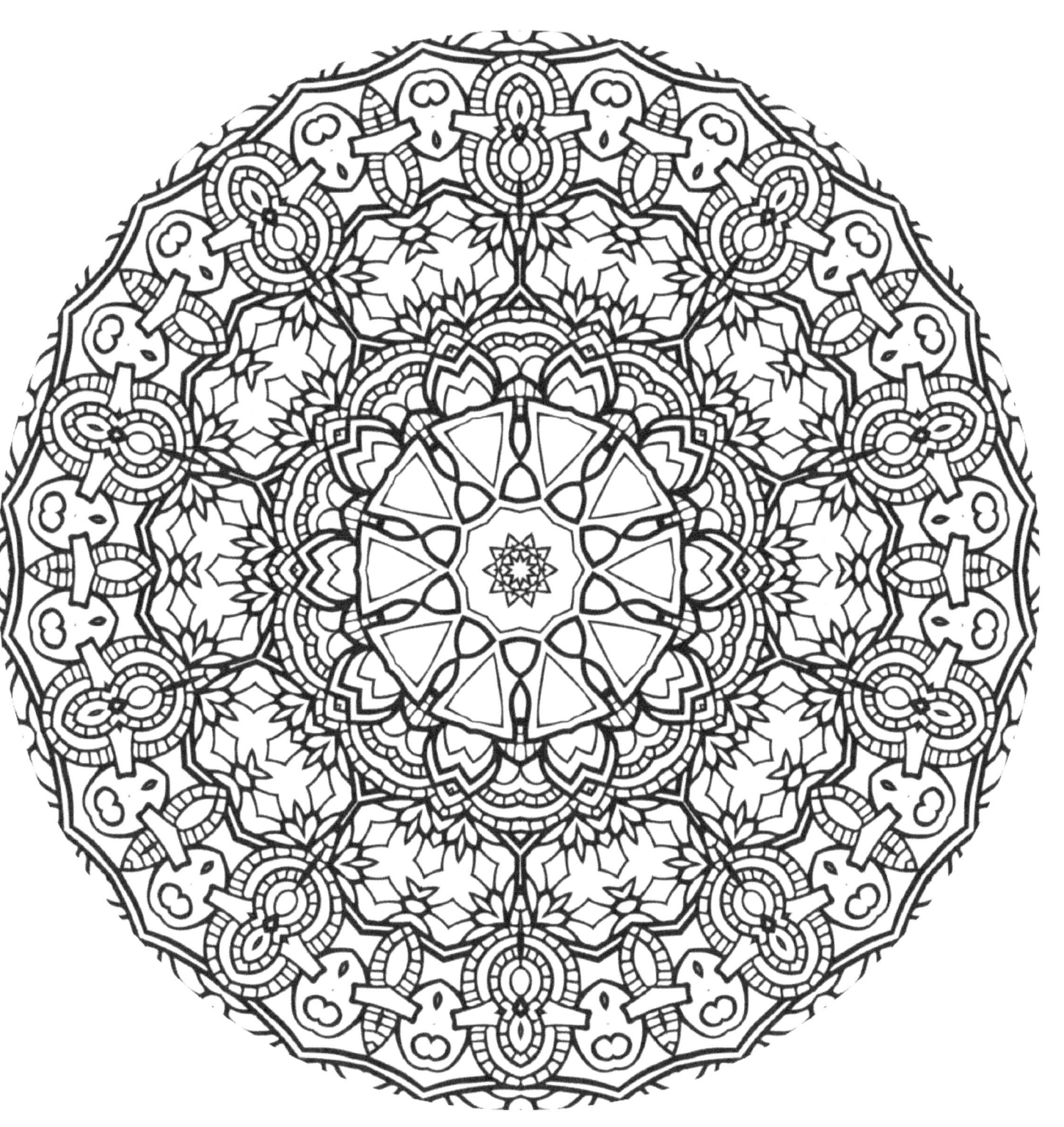

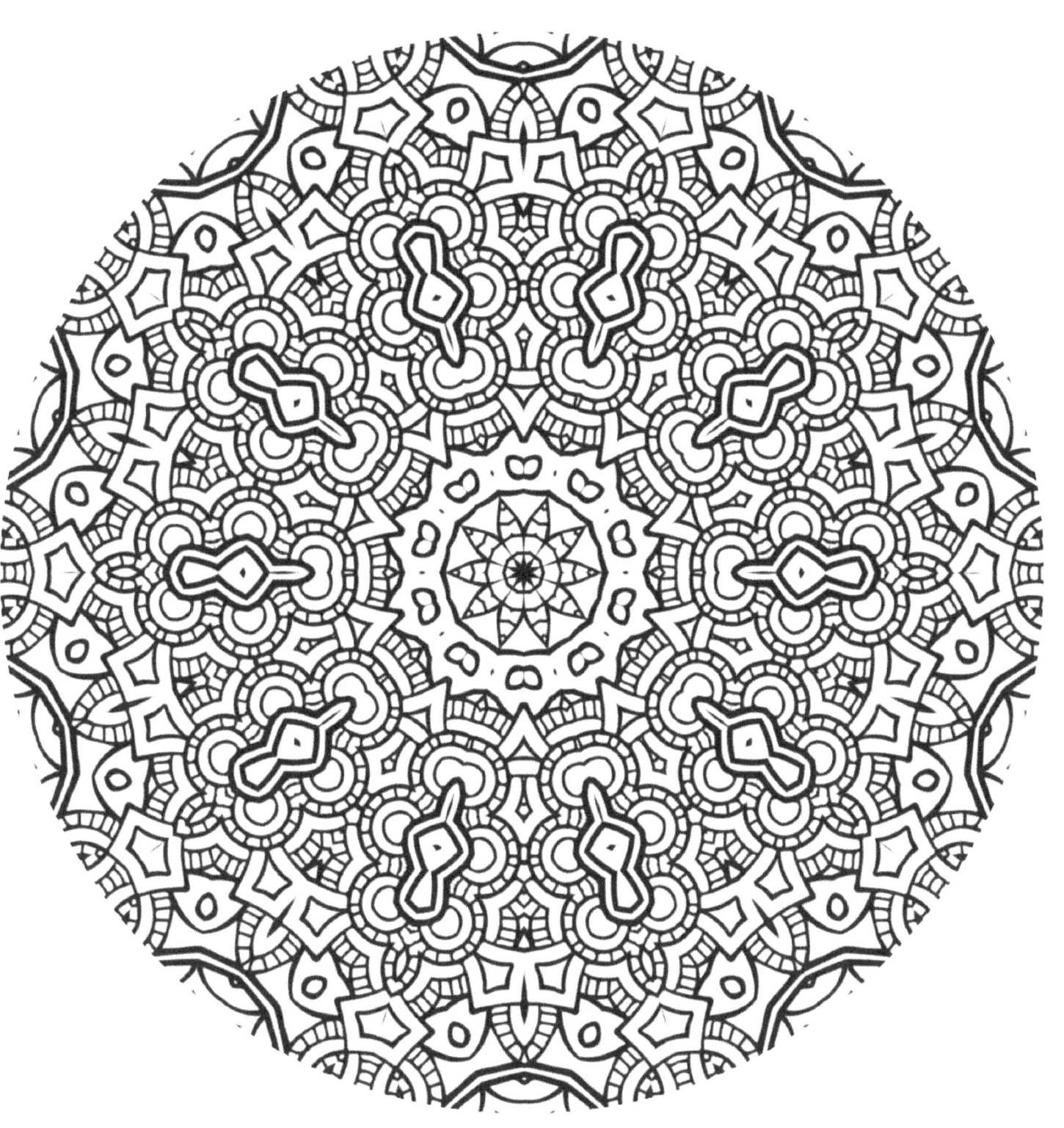

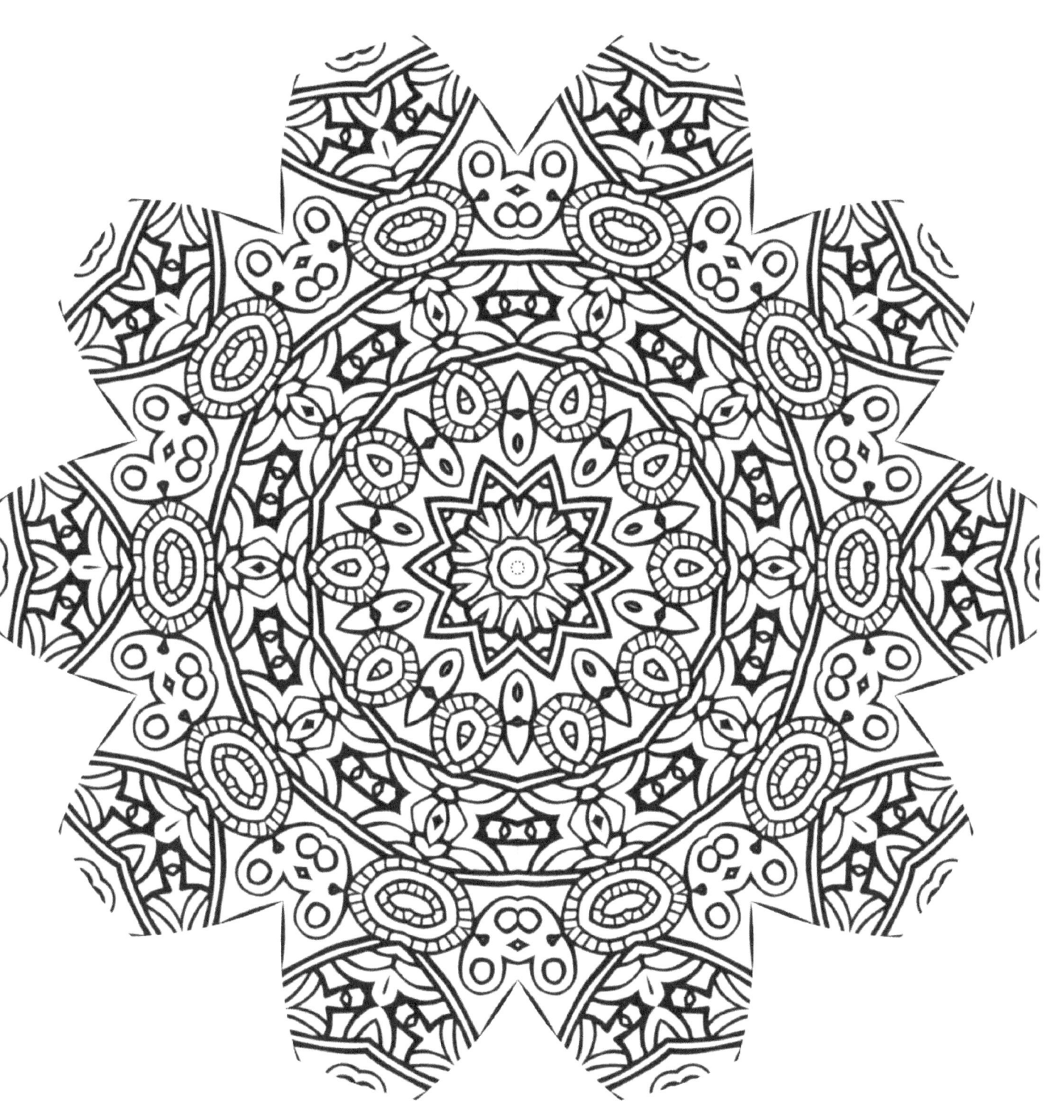

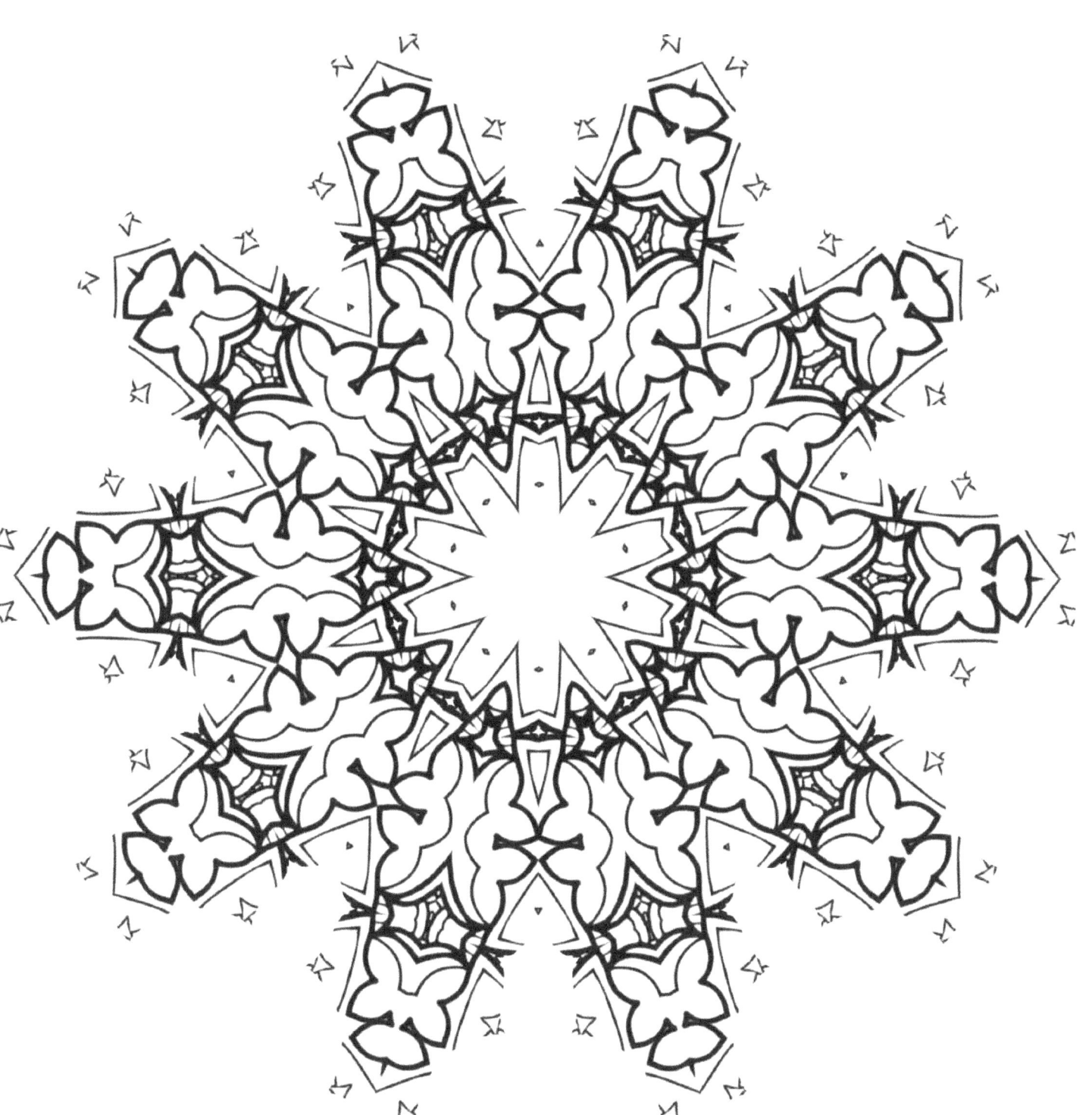

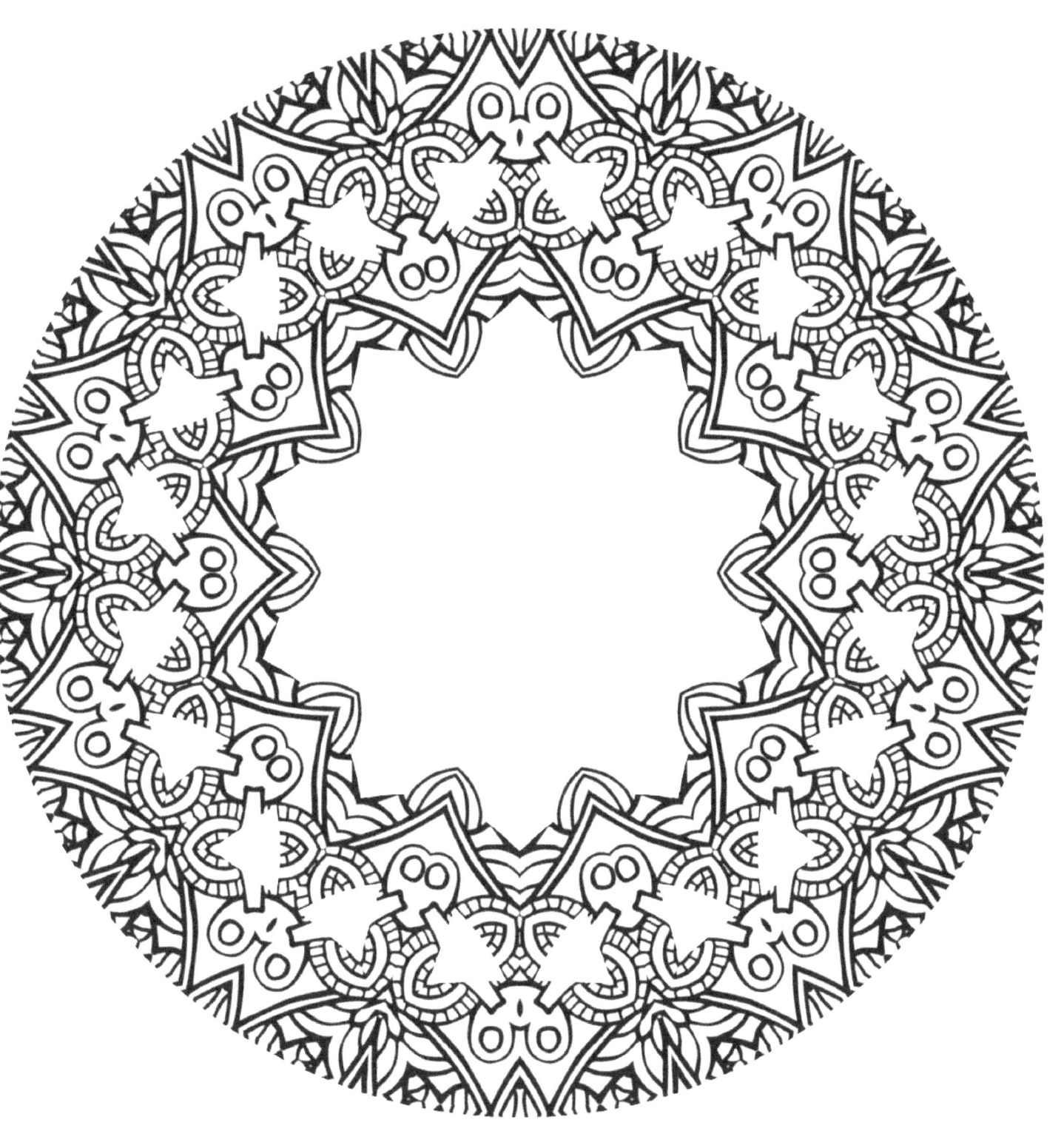

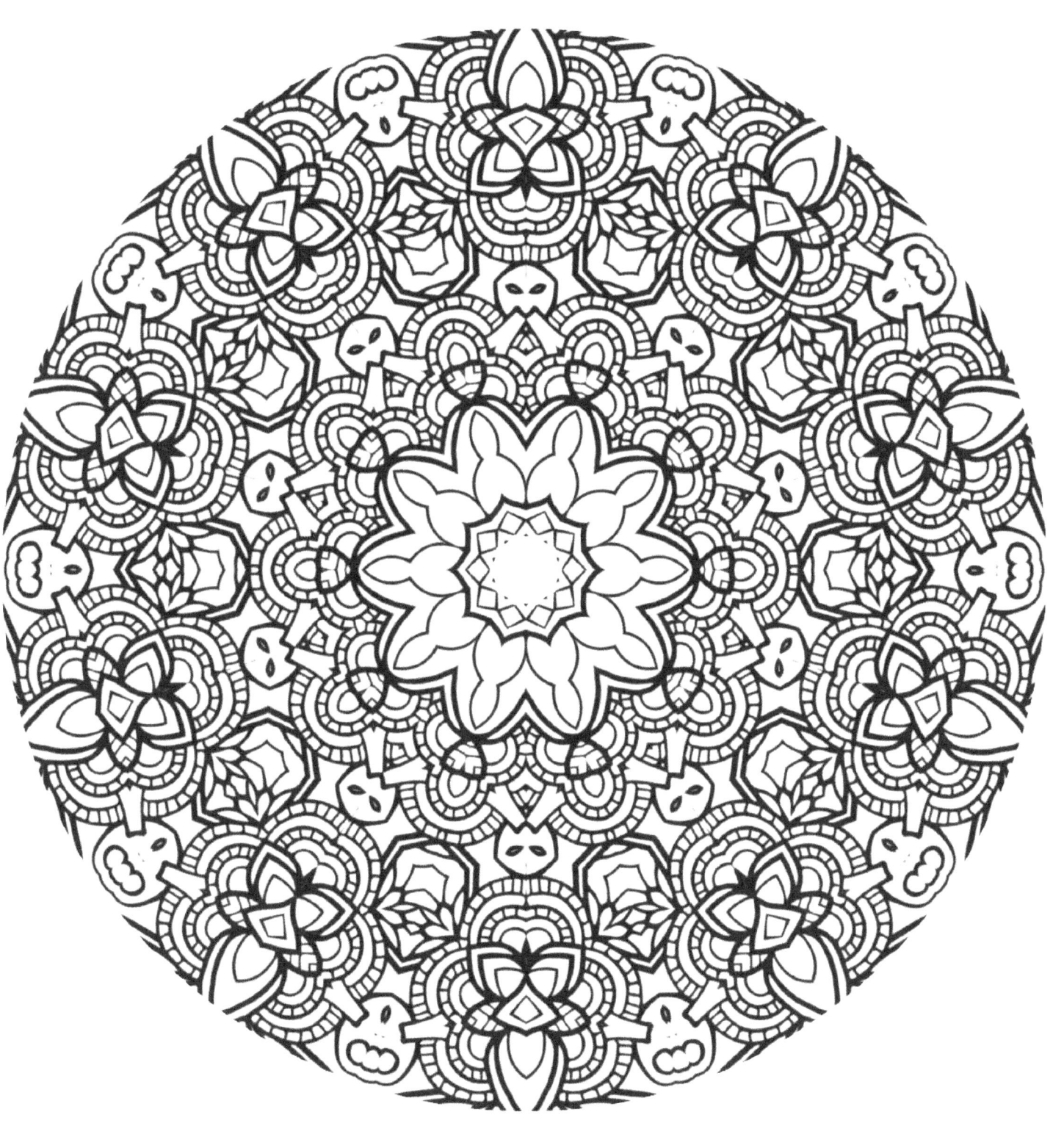

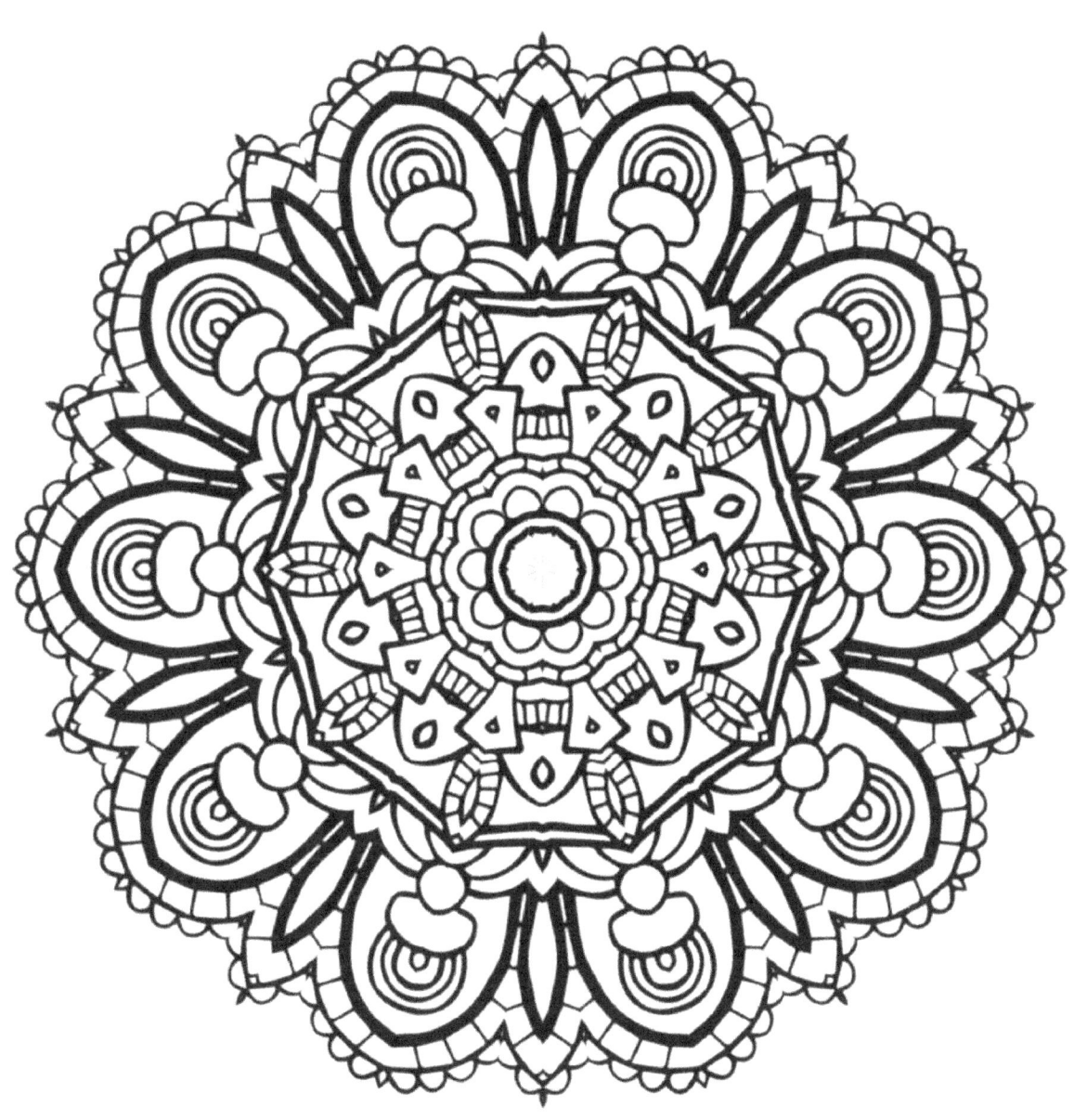

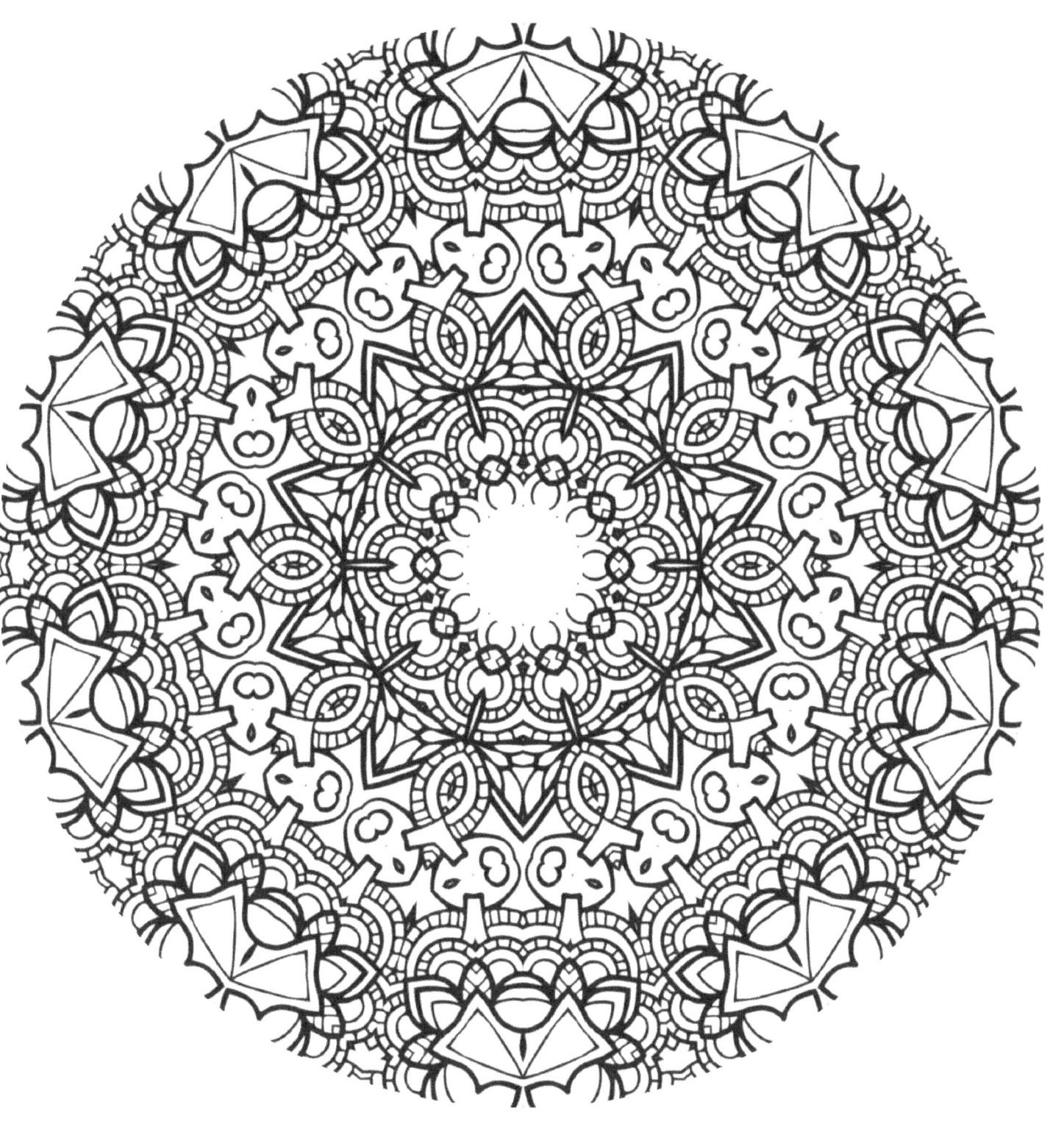

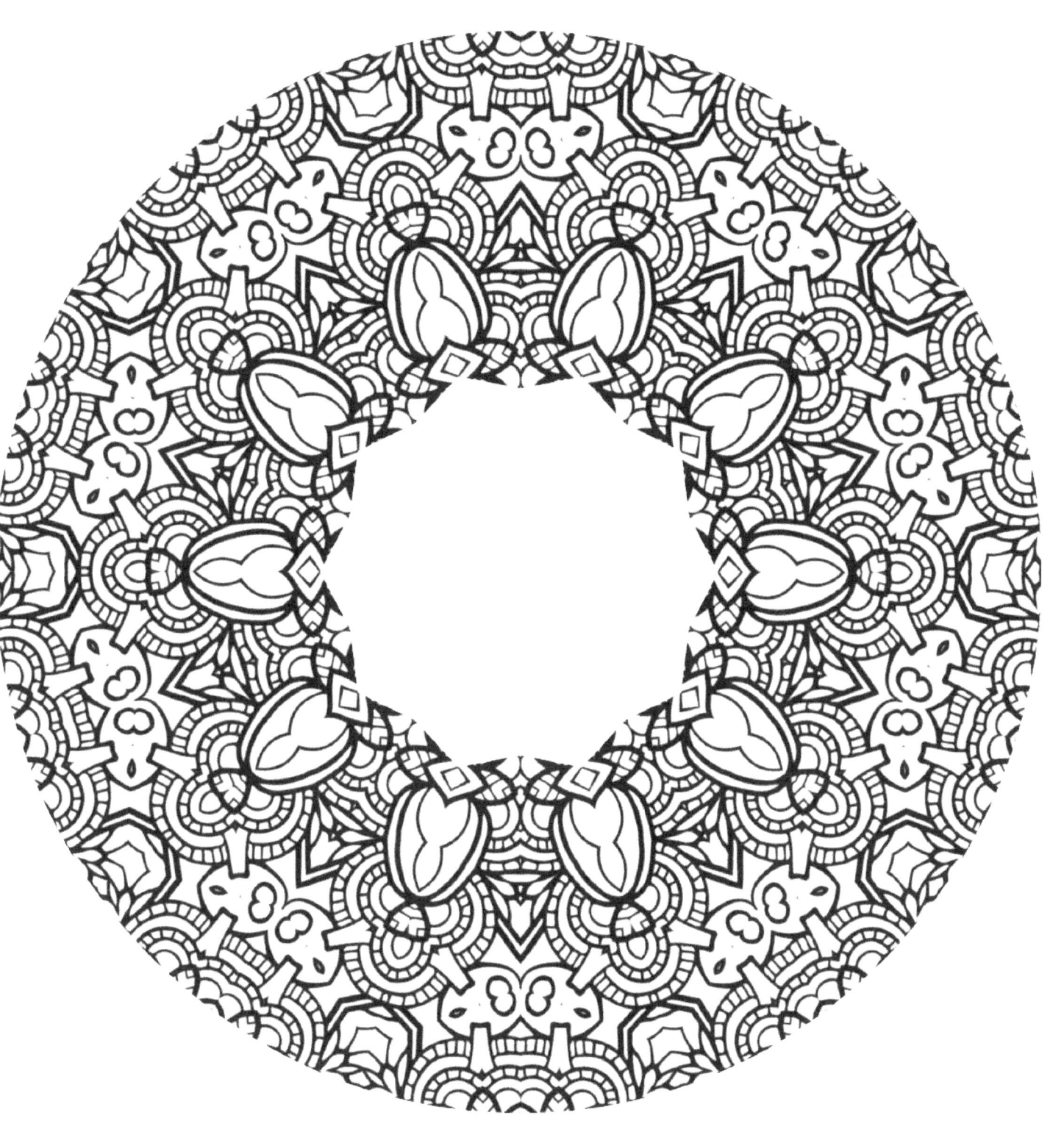

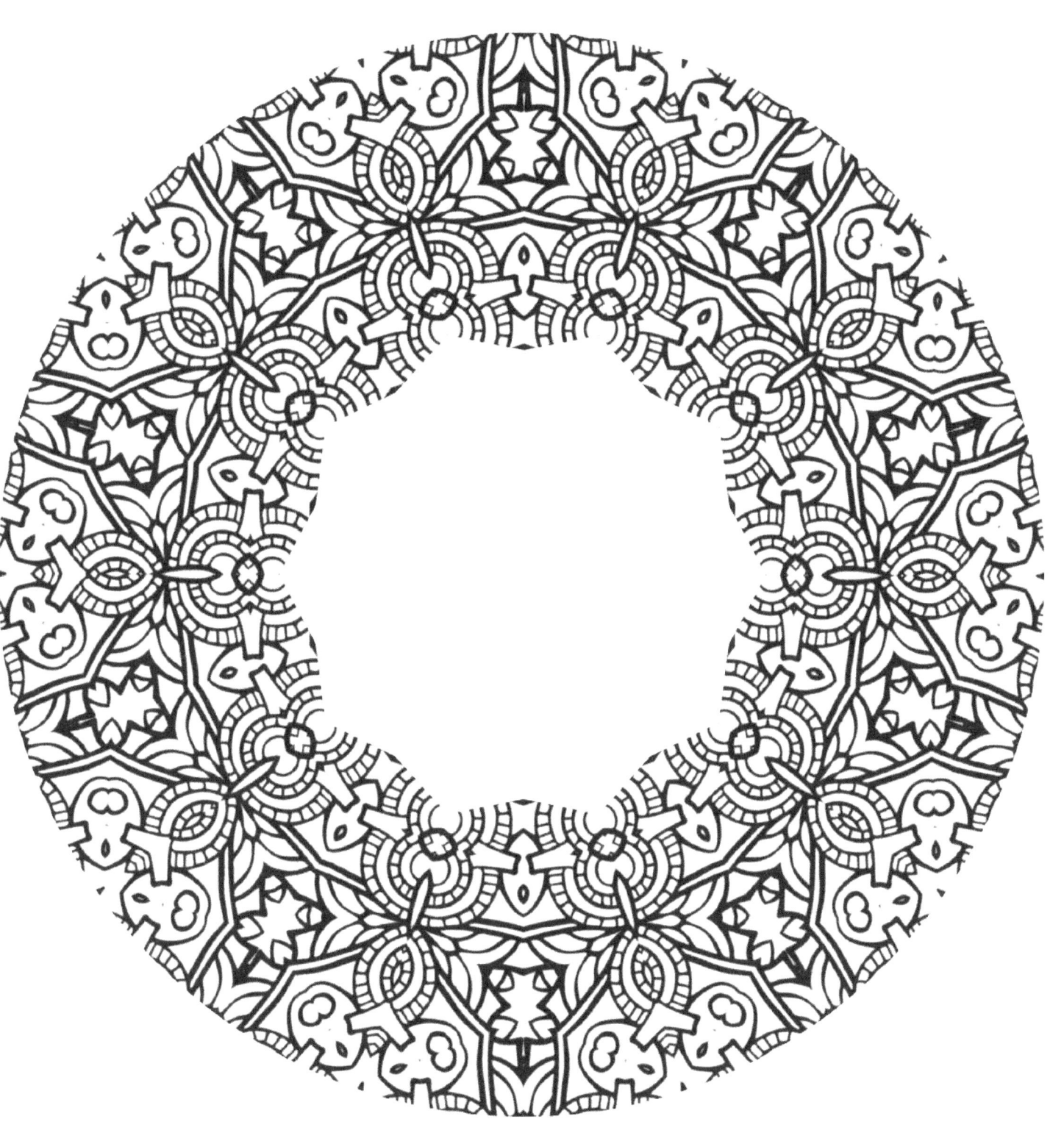

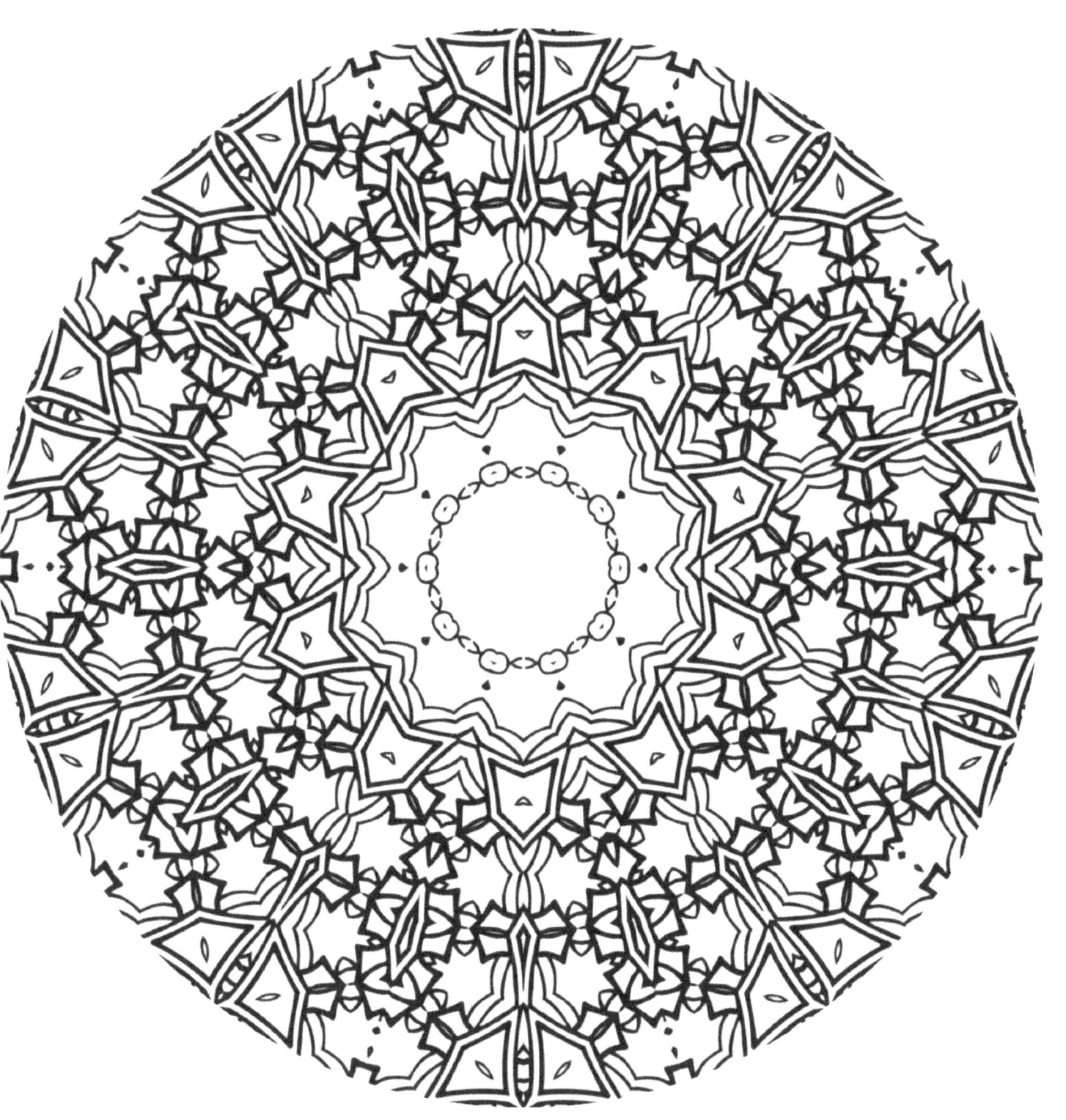

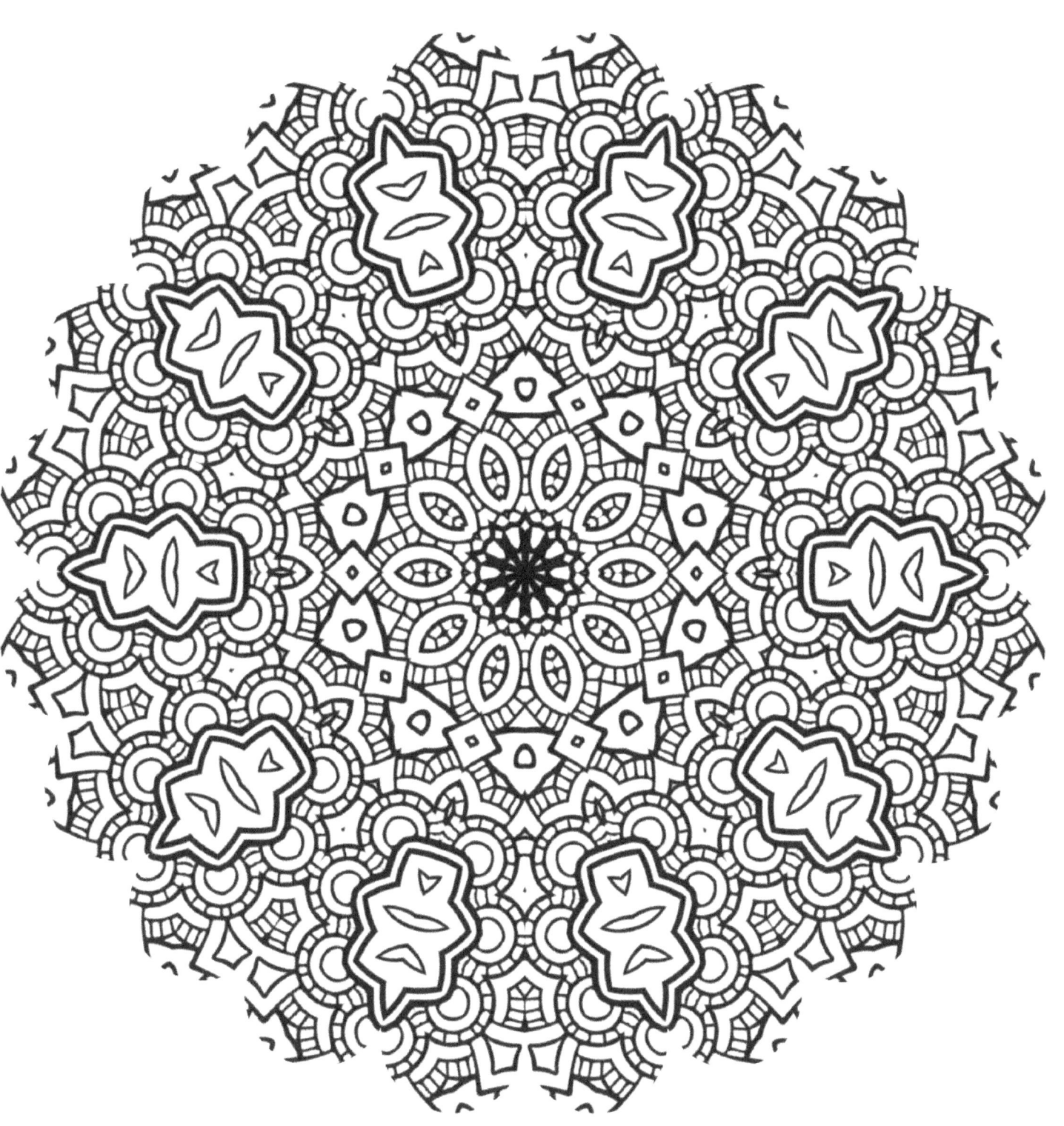

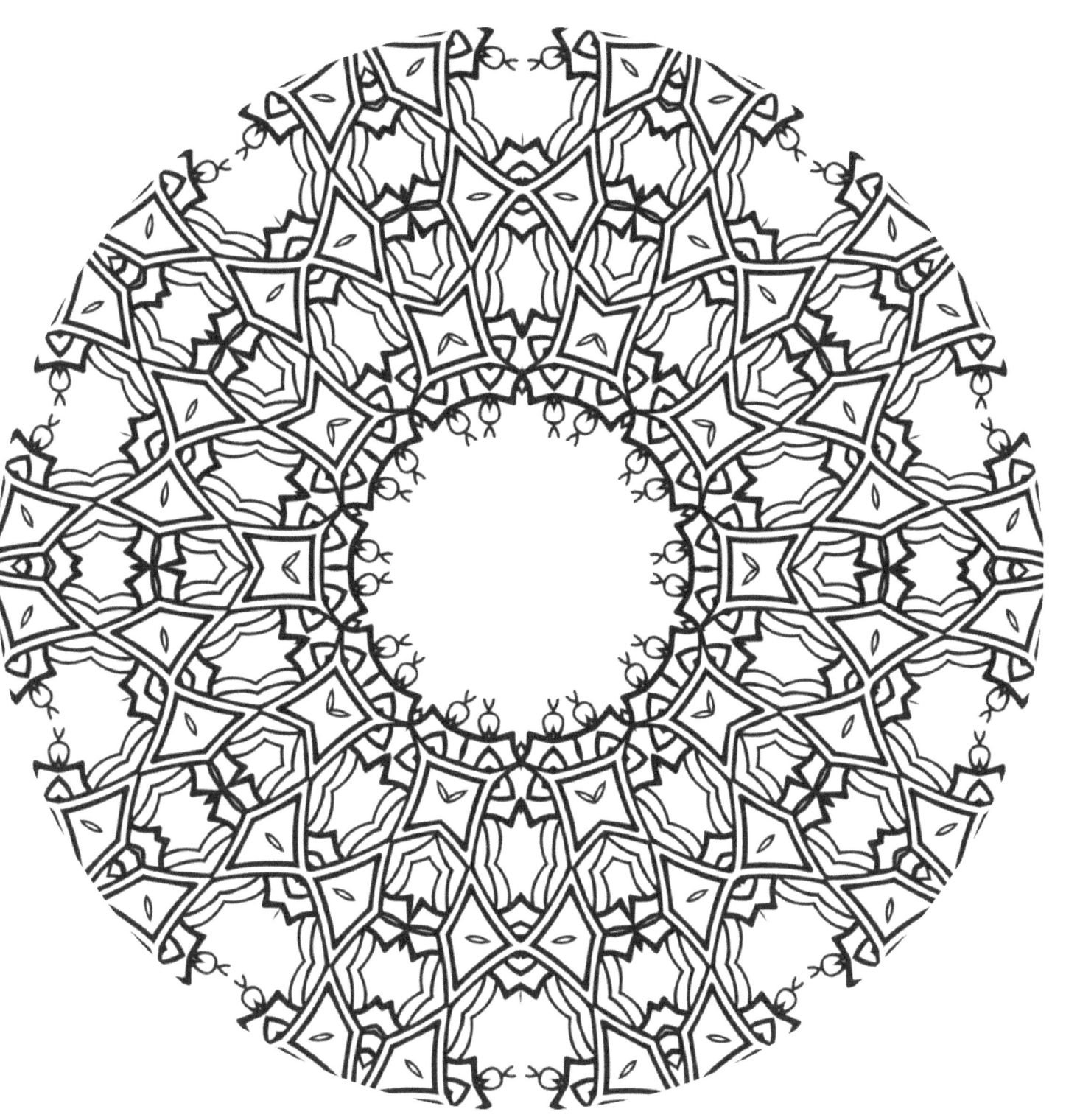

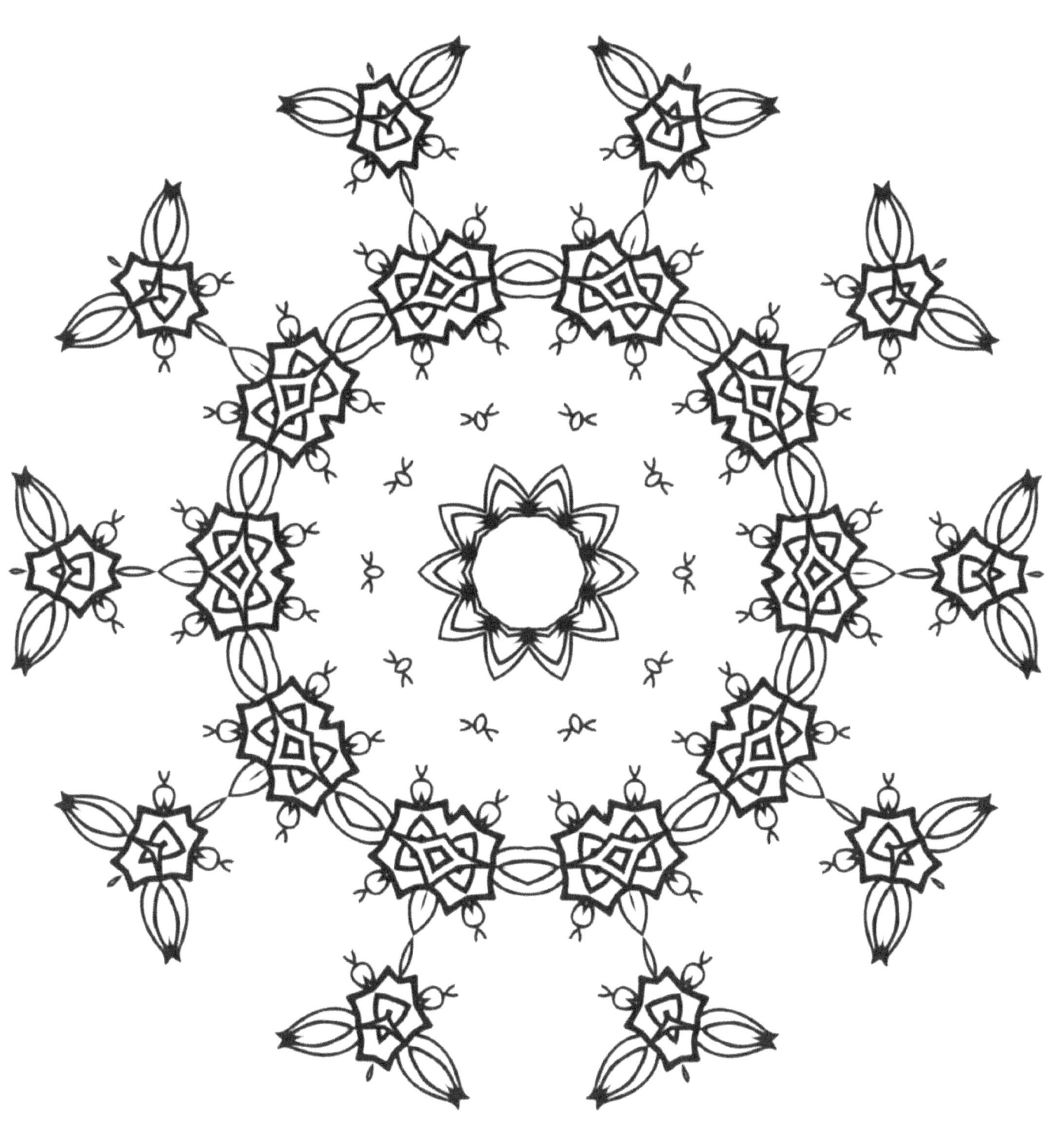

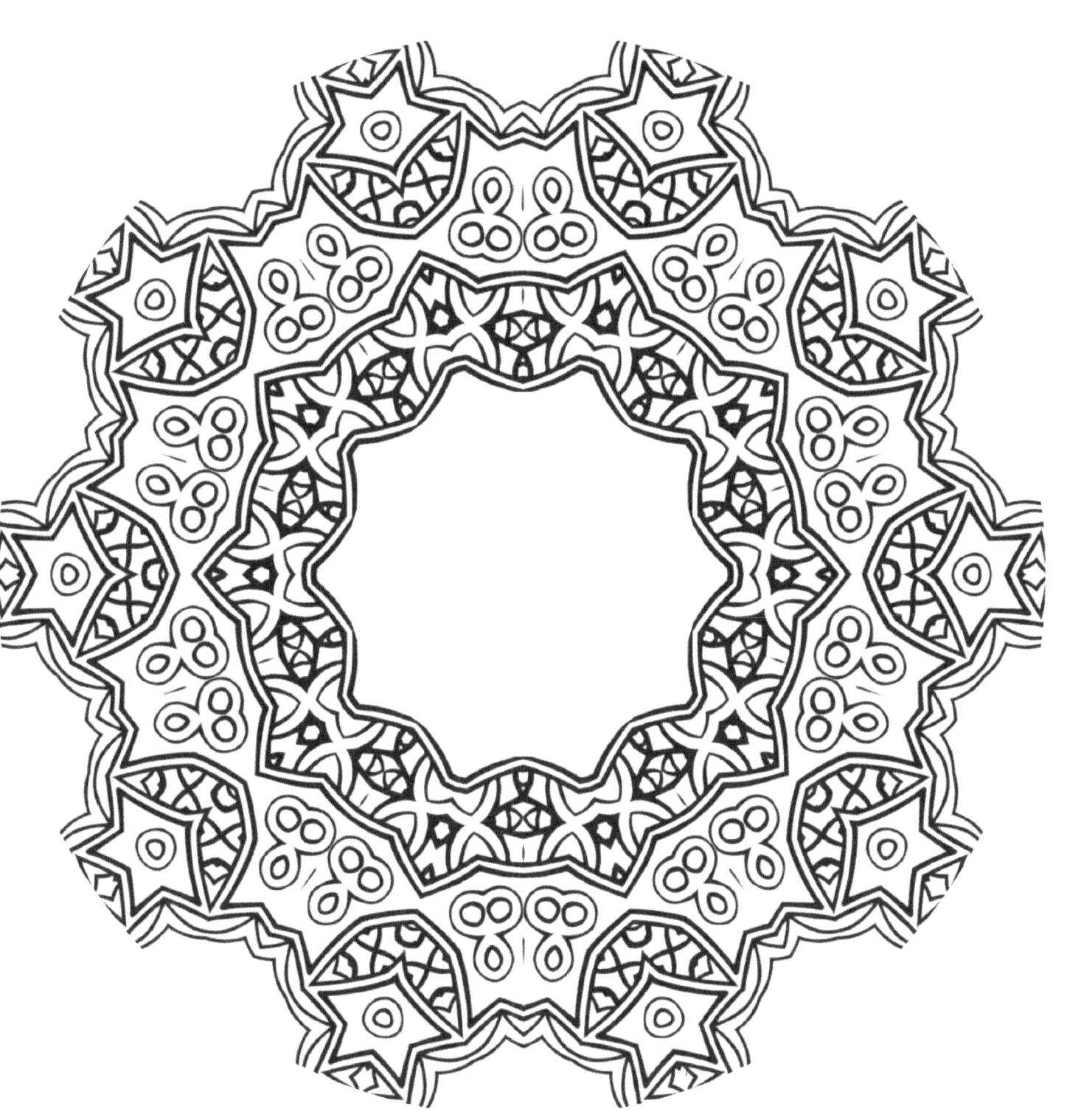

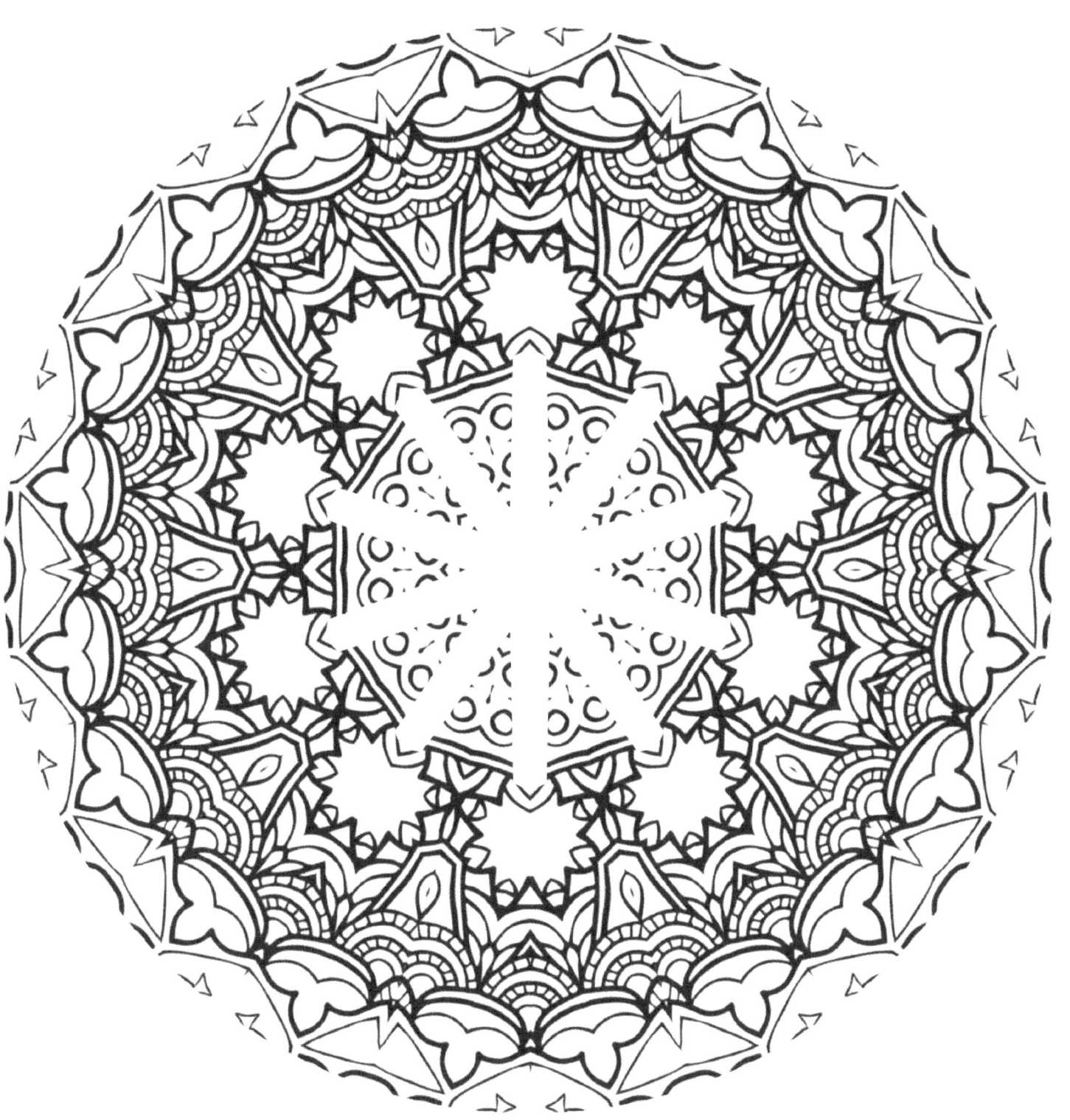

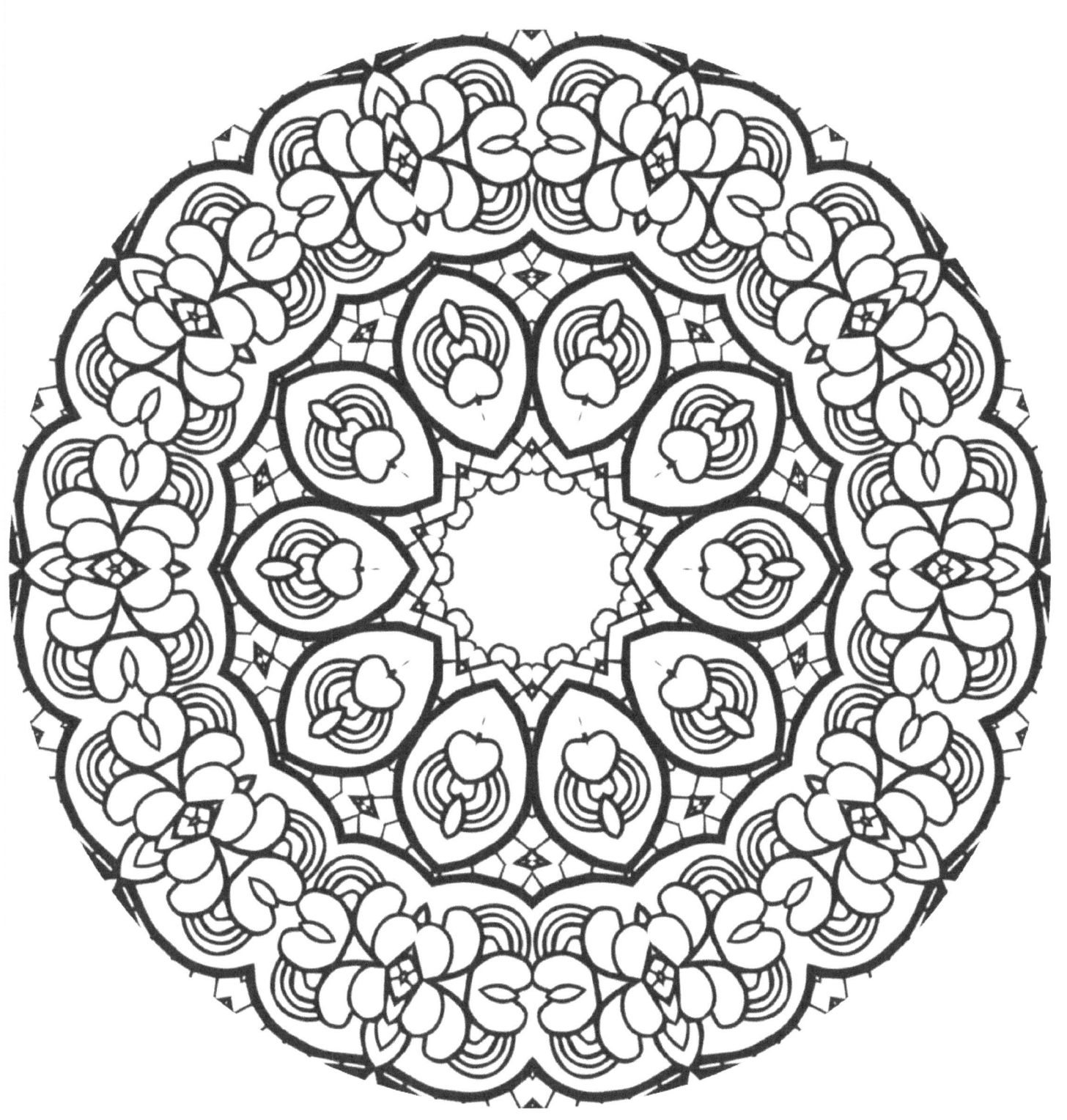

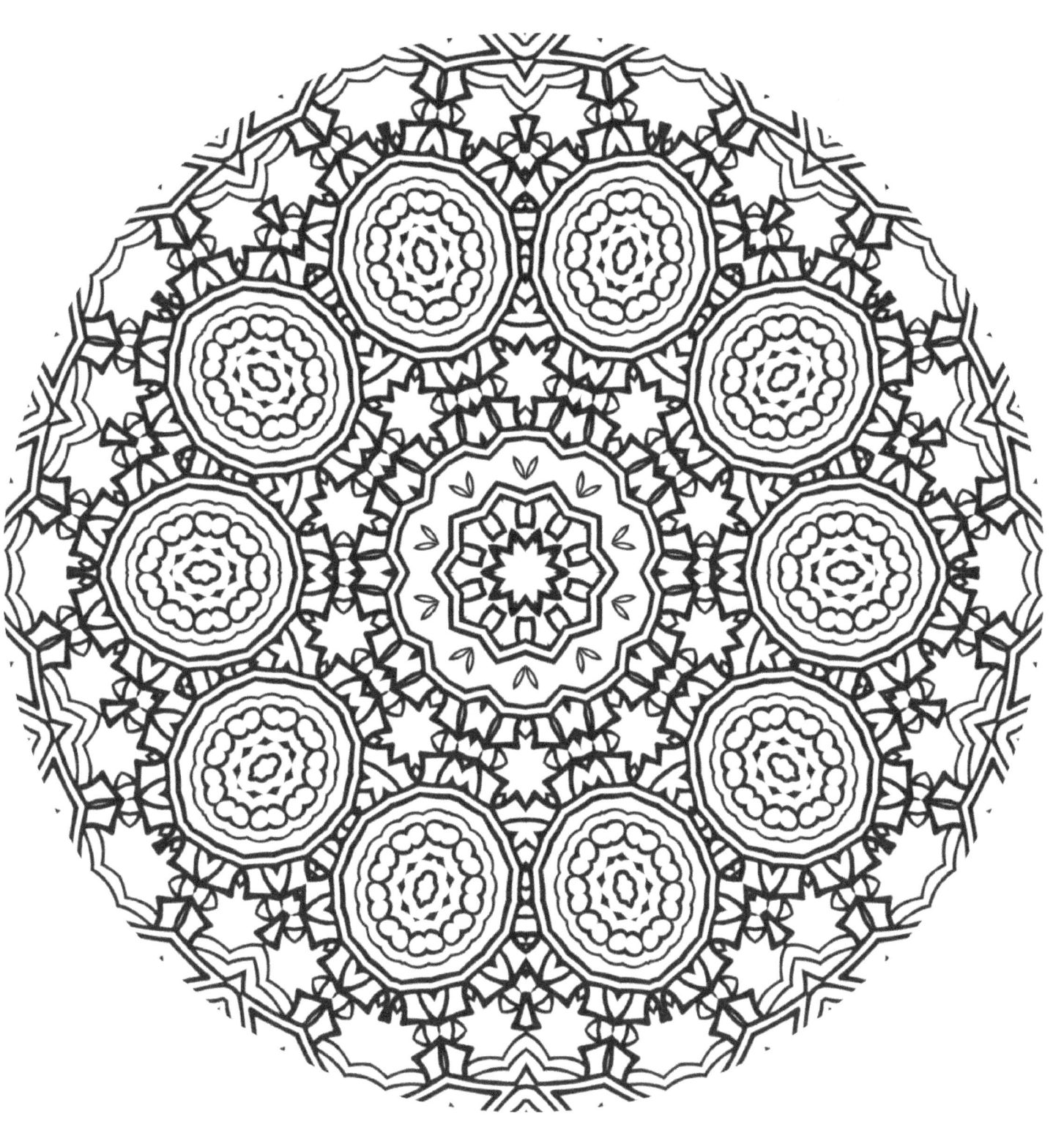

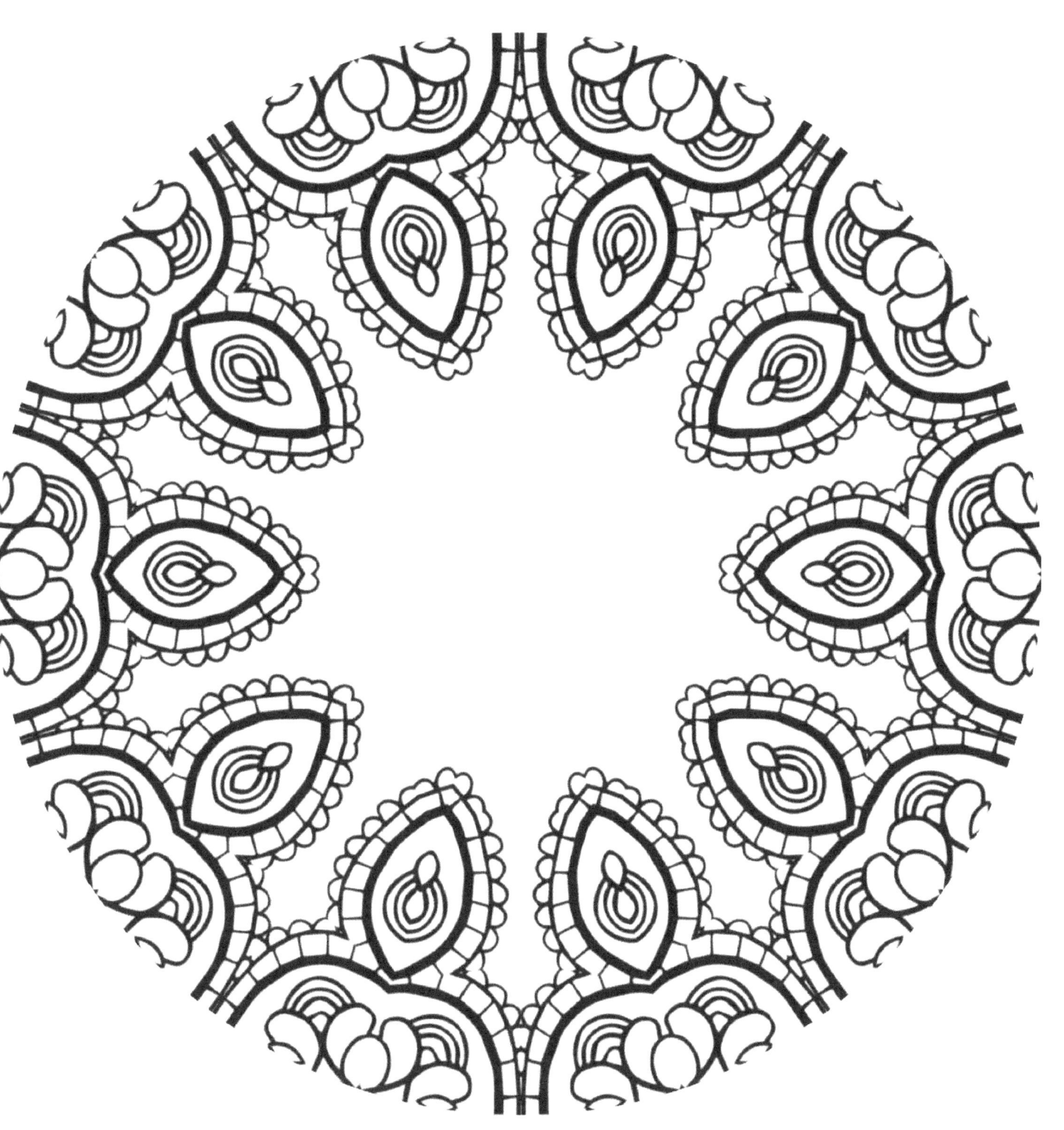

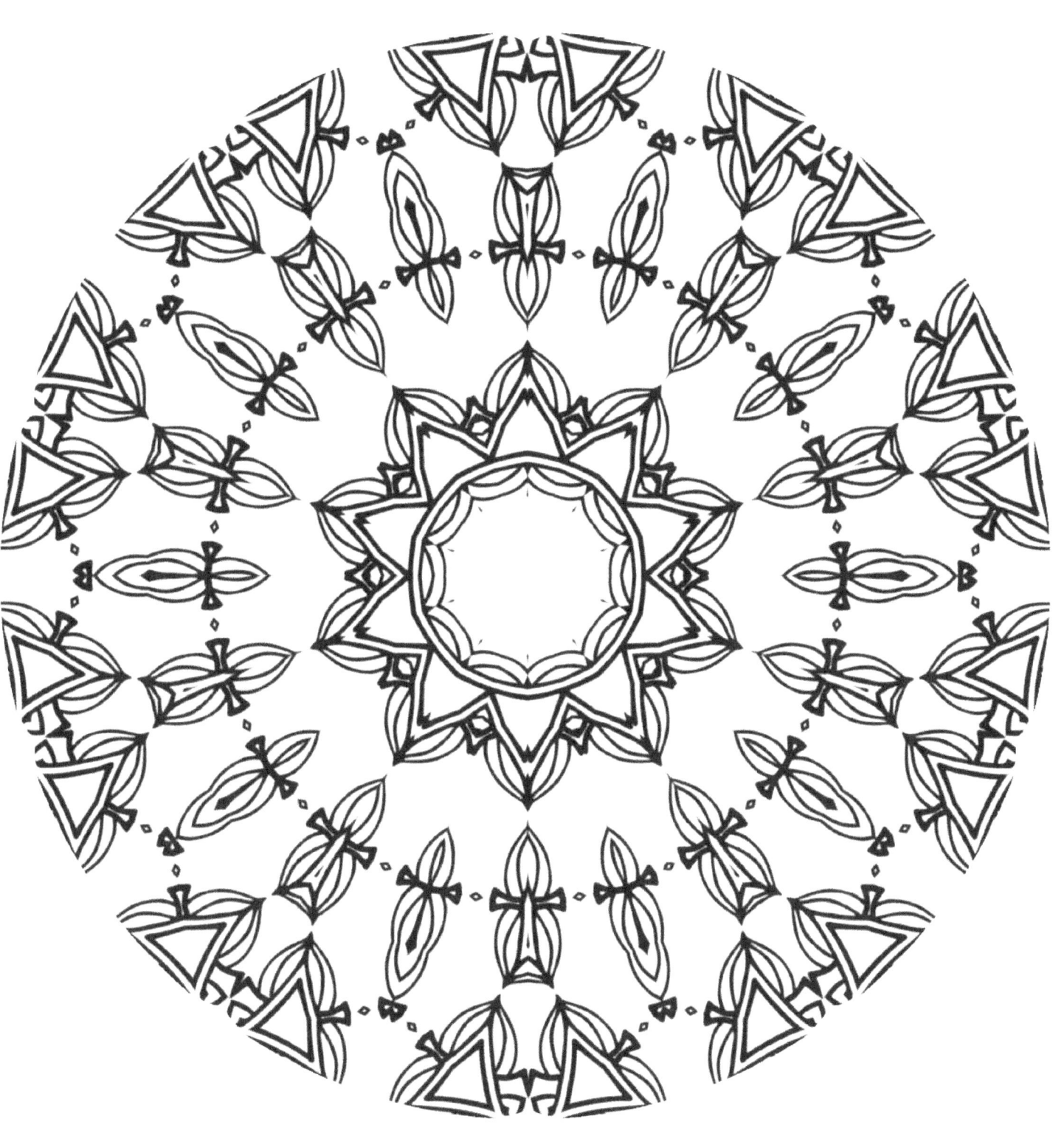

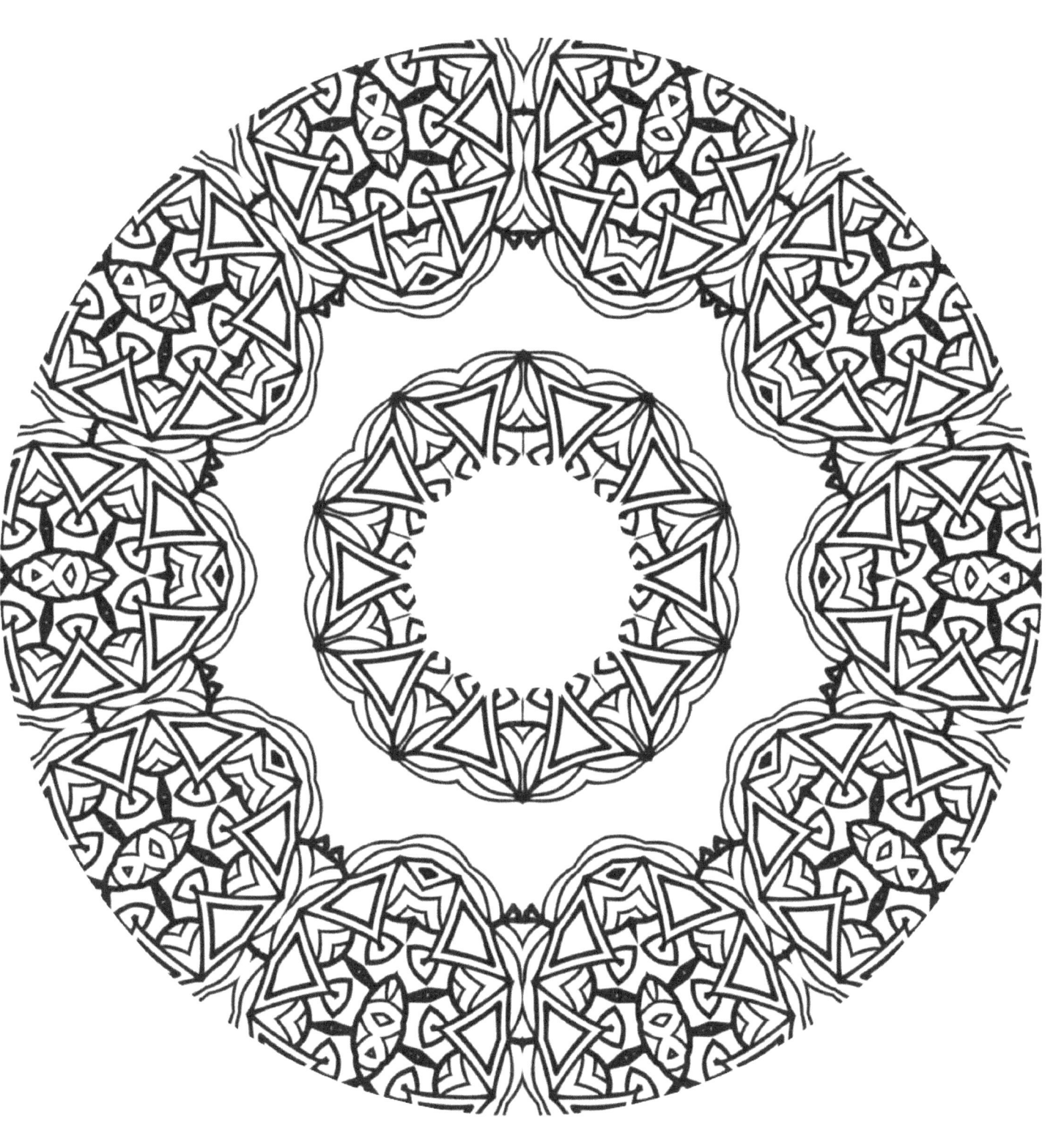

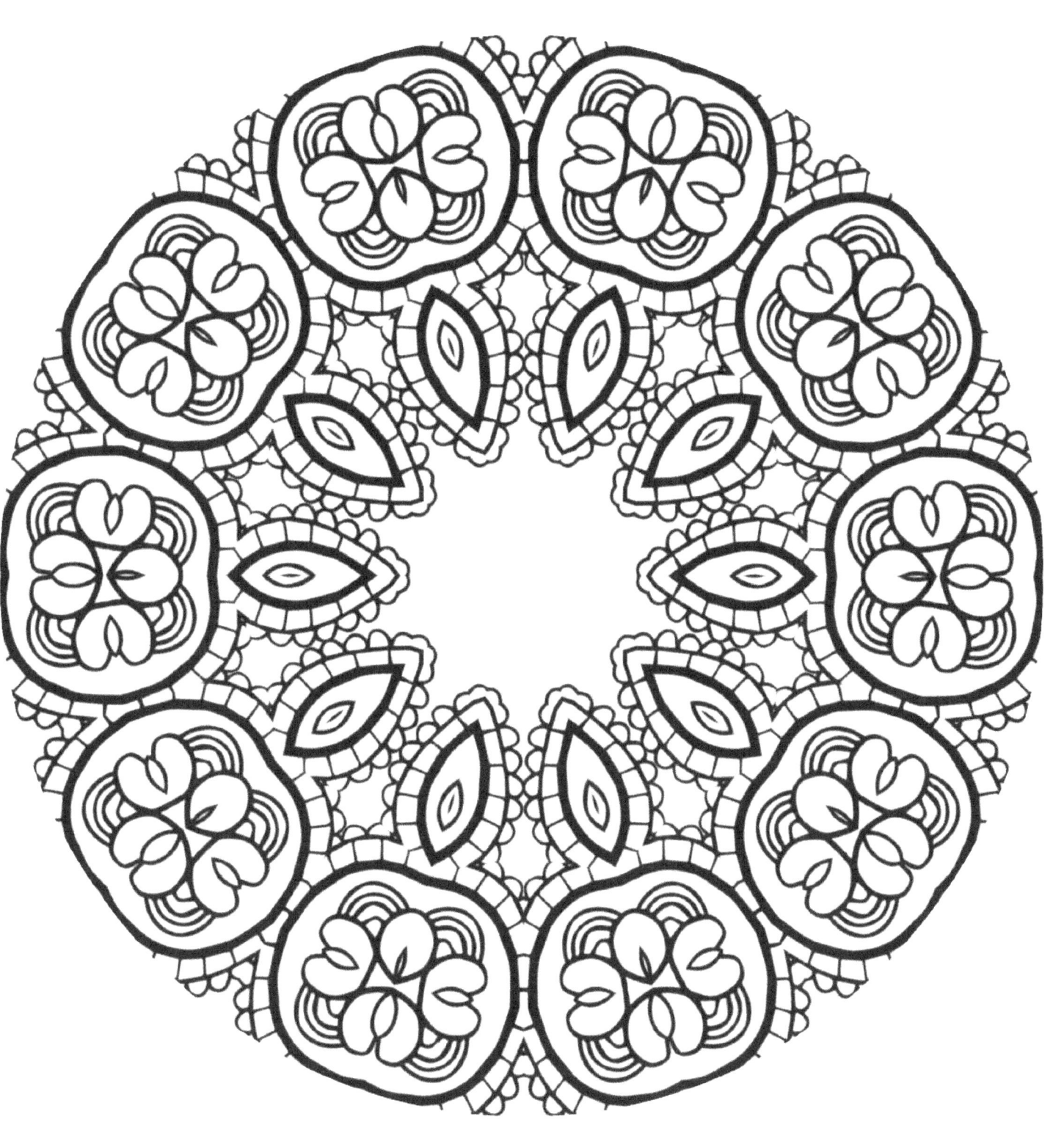

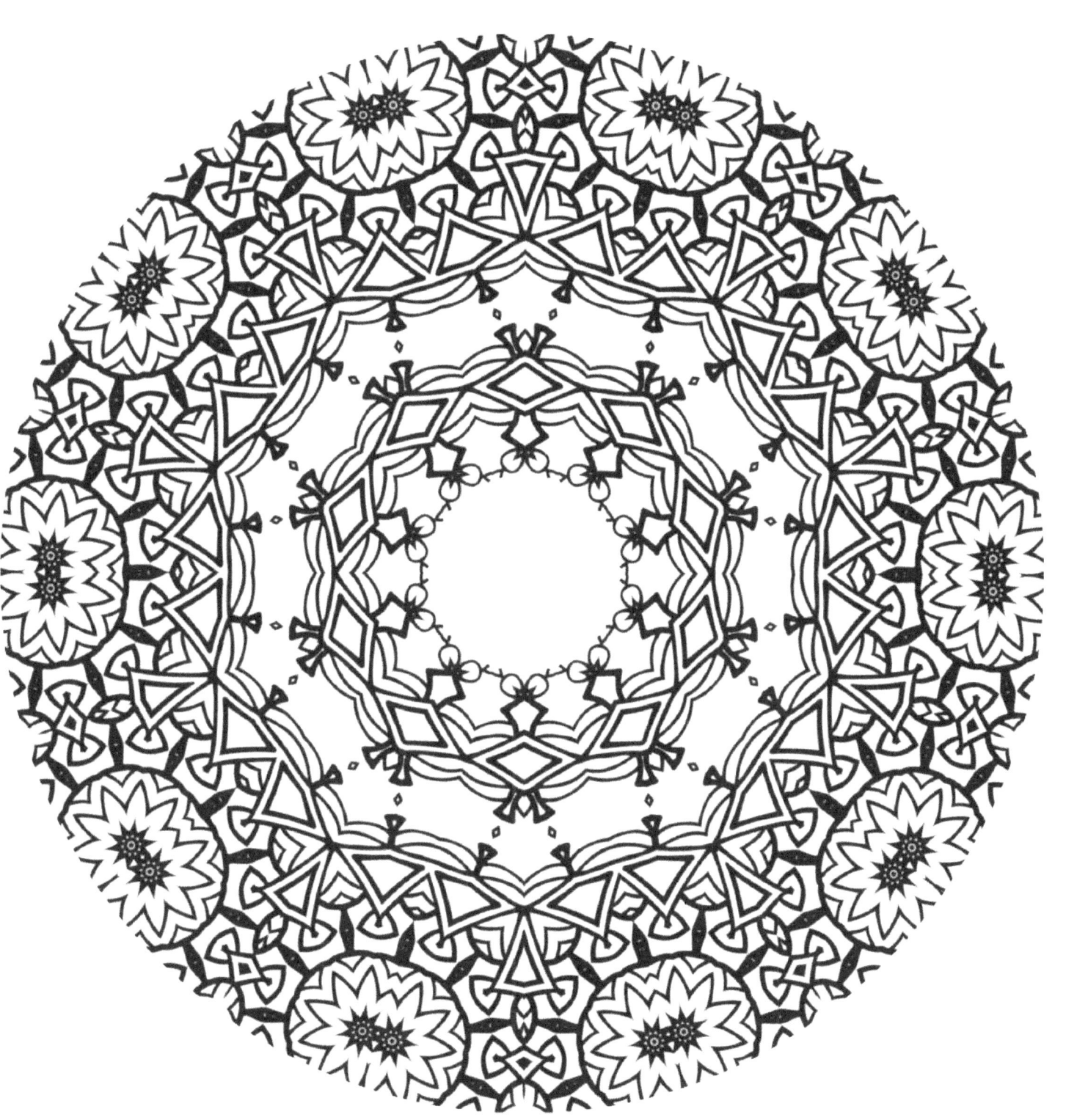

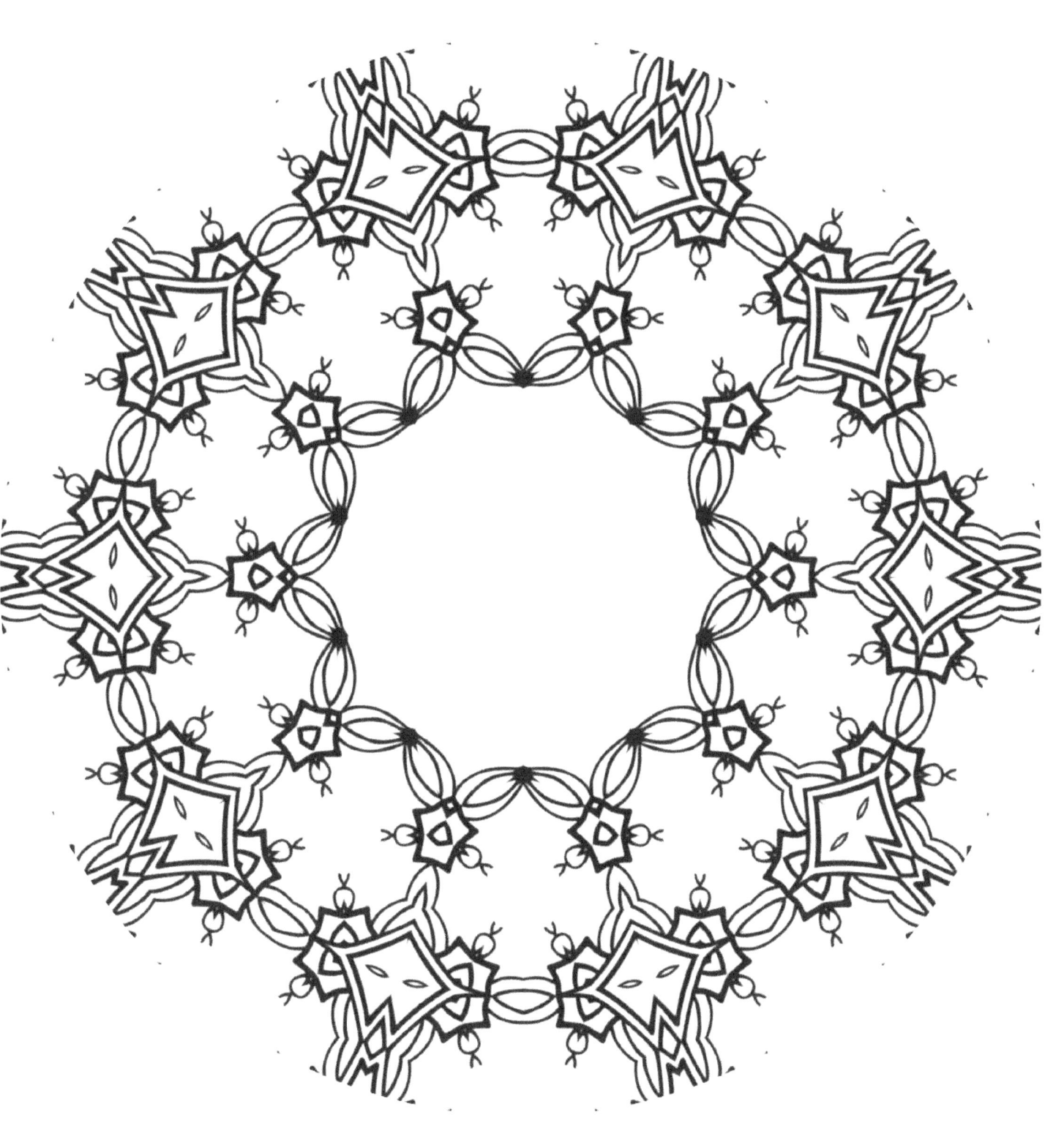

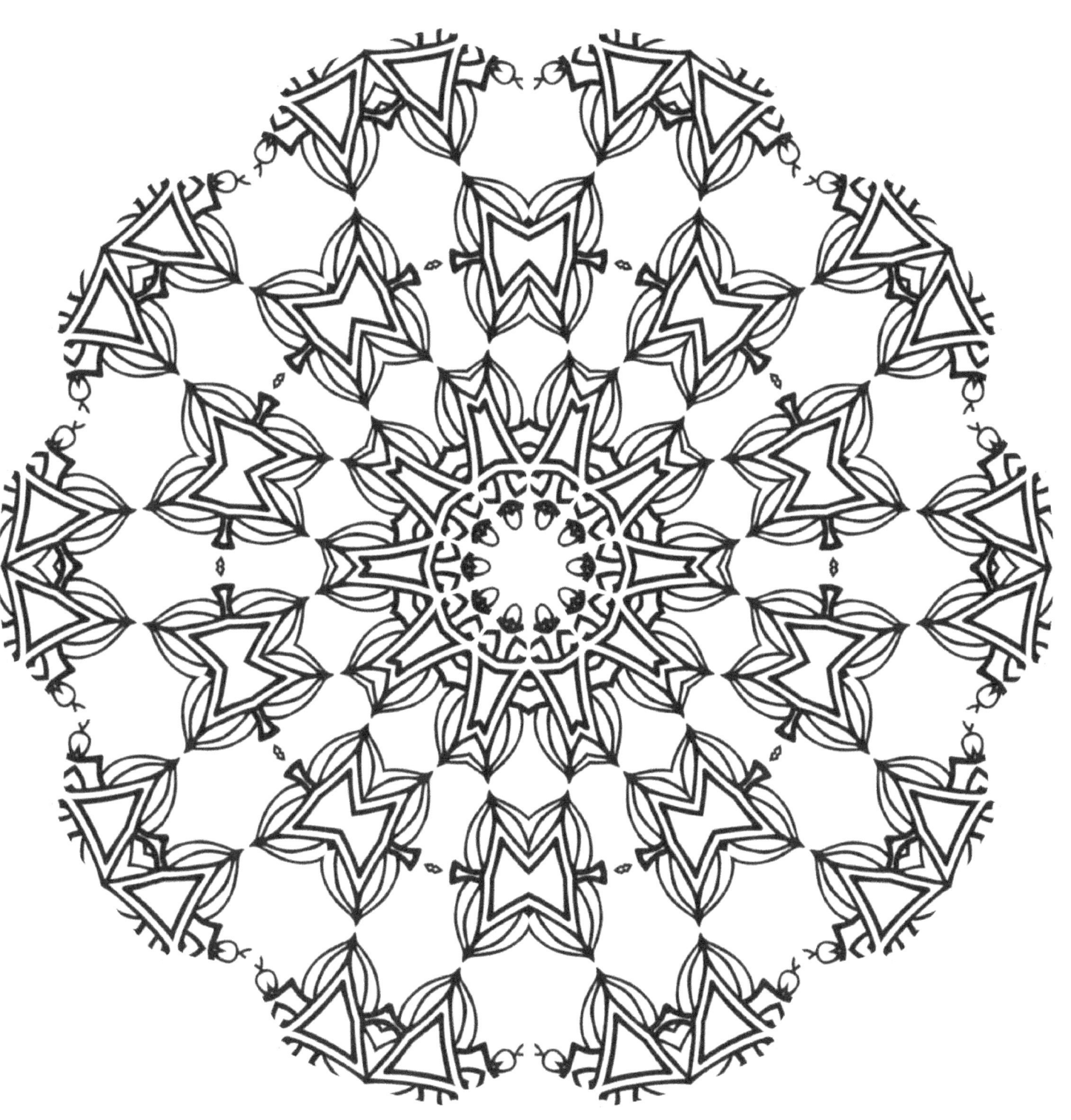

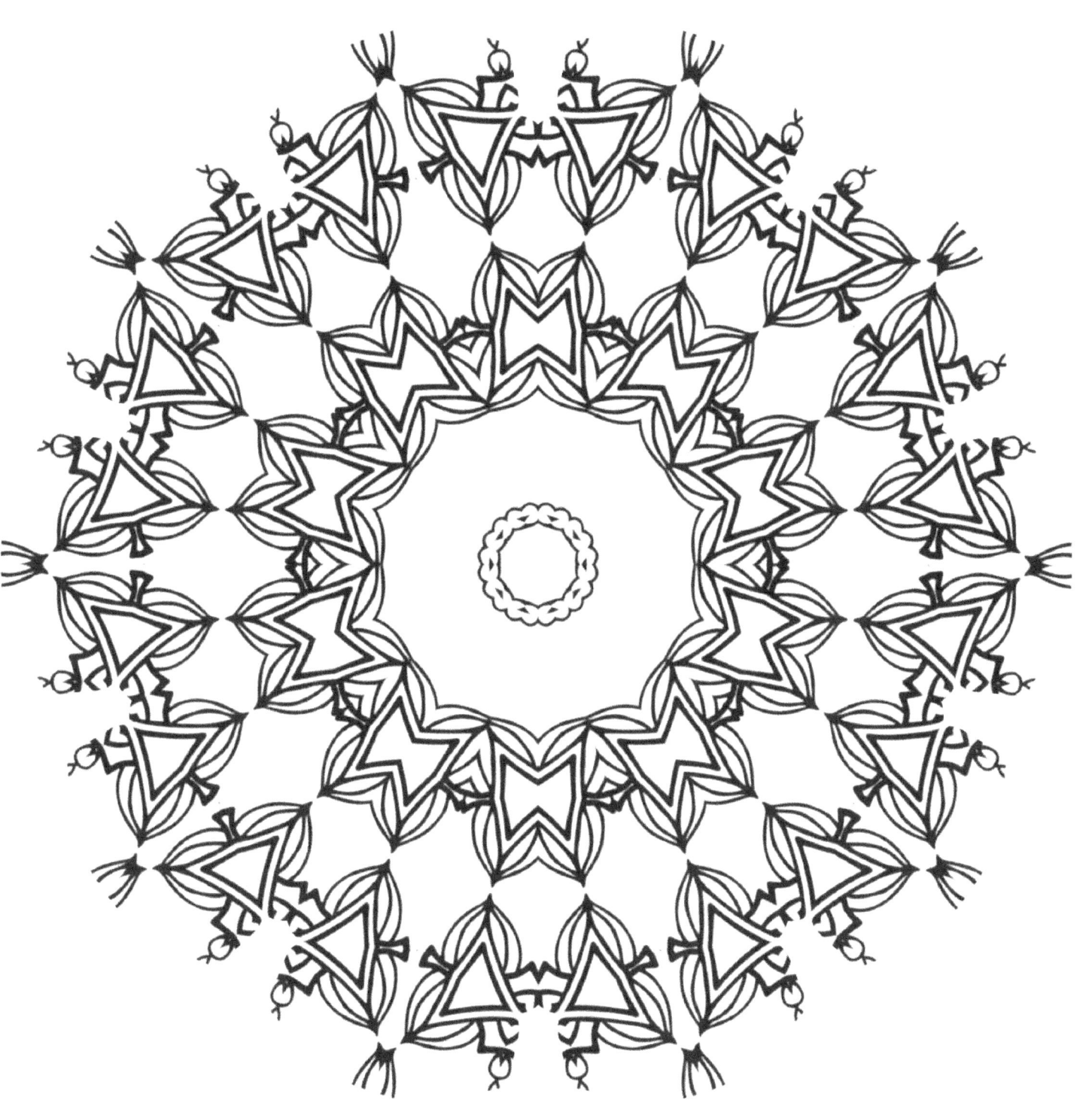

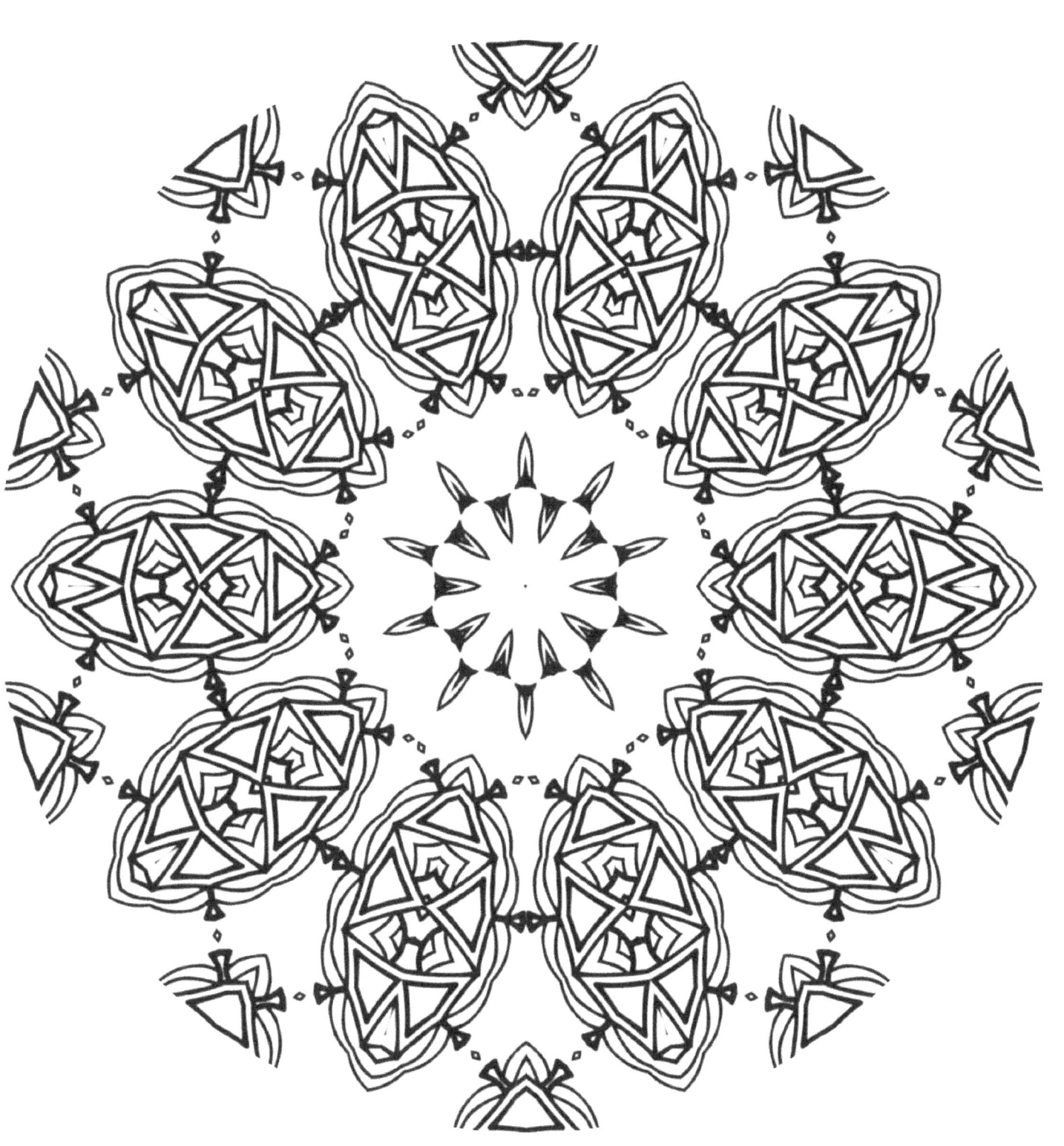

www.ingramcontent.com/pod-product-compliance
Lightning Source LLC
Chambersburg PA
CBHW081519220526
45467CB00010B/2979